IMAGES
of England

ROSSENDALE
THE SECOND SELECTION

Thomas, Joseph, Elizabeth and Emily Aston. Several members of the Aston family of Bacup have found their way on to the small screen. Among the roles played by the four family members pictured:

Emily led the way as Jess in *Oranges Are Not the Only Fruit*, since when she has also appeared in *Coronation Street* as Becky Palmer, *Children's Ward* as Sally and in various ITV dramas, besides several commercials.

Elizabeth (two years Emily's junior) played the role of Emmy-Lou in *Casualty* and Girl Guide in *You've Been Framed*.

Thomas (two years Elizabeth's junior) appeared as Colin in *The Bill*, Alex in *Peak Practice* and Mark in *Butterfly Collectors*.

Joseph (one year Thomas' junior) has appeared in several commercials, as well as playing Oscar in *Where the Heart is*, Harry Davies in *Heartbeat* and Tommy Duckworth in *Coronation Street*. He made his TV debut aged just four!

They are a credit to their native Bacup (photograph reproduced by courtesy of the *Lancashire Evening Telegraph*).

IMAGES
of England

ROSSENDALE
THE SECOND SELECTION

Ken Bowden

TEMPUS

First published 2002
Copyright © Ken Bowden, 2002

Tempus Publishing Limited
The Mill, Brimscombe Port,
Stroud, Gloucestershire, GL5 2QG

ISBN 0 7524 2477 7

Typesetting and origination by
Tempus Publishing Limited
Printed in Great Britain by
Midway Colour Print, Wiltshire

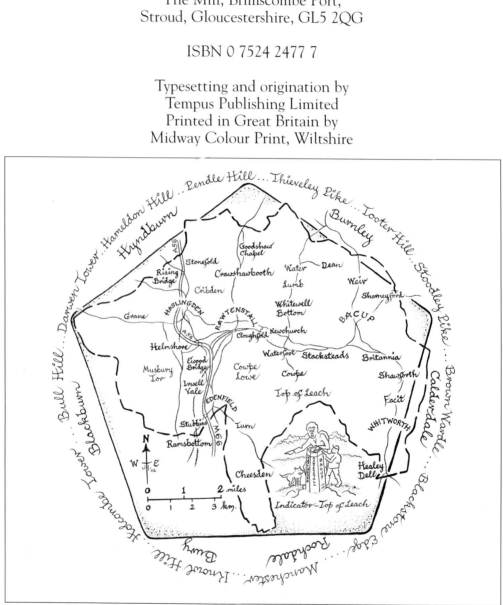

Five-sided sketch of Rossendale to match the five-sided stone pillar at the summit of Top of Leach, 1,555ft above sea level. Erected in 1974 to mark local government reorganisation, it stands near the point where four of the five former districts join, with each of the five sides engraved with the name of that former district. The pointer on the top indicates surrounding landmarks such as those cited round the edges of this sketch.

Contents

Acknowledgements   6

Introduction   7

1.   Whitworth and its Valley   9

2.   Bacup   17

3.   Stacksteads and Wolfenden Areas   35

4.   Musical Interlude   63

5.   Rawtenstall and Points North   73

6.   Stubbins, Edenfield and Rossendale West
     (including Haslingden)   95

The Rossendale Sunday School Union was founded on New Year's Day 1844 at Waterbarn Baptist School, Stacksteads, attended by six Baptist schools, with two United Methodist schools (Bethesda and Waterside) joining later that year. In 1890 Mr James S. Hardman became secretary and played a major role in the Union, initiating scripture and temperance examinations and in 1898 an annual Eisteddfod, with H.W. Trickett (later Sir Henry) donating a shield for the best Sunday School choir. In 1917 central offices were opened at 49 Kay Street, Rawtenstall, and to mark the sesquicentenary of the first Sunday School the Union opened its own bookroom at 217 Bacup Road, Cloughfold. At this time fifty-six Sunday Schools were affiliated to the Rossendale Sunday School Union, comprising 1,637 teachers and 10,617 scholars. Though Sunday School members are now down to twenty, the Rossendale Sunday School Union still functions. Raikes House is still there, but was vacated by the Union around 1970.

Introduction and Acknowledgements

In this second selection of pictures representing Rossendale, I have tried to highlight some of the areas that often seem to be overlooked – amongst them Shawforth, Scout, Strongstry and Stonefold, all of which are represented by at least a couple of pictorial inclusions. I have also tried, with a mere handful of exceptions, to exclude items that have been previously published in books.

I am grateful for the opportunity to include a good number from the local collections of libraries in the area. For which my thanks to Lancashire County Library and the ever-helpful librarians of Accrington, Bacup, Haslingden, Rawtenstall and Whitworth. Sandra Cruise and the staff of Whitaker Park Museum have also been exceedingly generous in making pictorial material available to me.

I am particularly grateful to the three wise men (at least) from Haslingden who have done their best to ensure that my notes about that area of Rossendale are reasonably accurate – Tom Fisher, John Simpson and Donald Valentine, not forgetting Alec Taylor.

I am indebted to Mrs Edna Kirby for allowing me the use of her own photographs and those taken by her father Arthur Constantine, arguably Haslingden's best-known photographer.

Involvement in recent years with Bacup Natural History Society has turned up some rare specimens which I am delighted to be able to include, among them some definite 'characters'. Thanks to Ben Ashworth, Harry O'Neill and Ken Simpson for advice, comments and encouragement. The same is true of the members of Whitworth Historical Society, who have likewise turned up several treasures for my inspection and use.

I have chosen to begin with the Whitworth Valley and work in a gradually westerly direction, ending up on the Hyndburn boundary, with a breather in the middle where a 'Musical Interlude' may awaken a few chords of memory: 'If music be the food of love, play on...' – or *sing* on, if you prefer.

Any apparent imbalance in this compilation is incidental and not deliberate. There is certainly enough photographic material around illustrating Rossendale past and present for more publications of this nature. Any single individual's choice of pictures to include is likely to be rather different from another's.

I gladly acknowledge the help given by the Rossendale Free Press and its editor who have made several of their photographs available. In addition I must record my thanks to Jeffrey Altham for access to Newchurch scouting records, Arthur Baldwin, Arnold Barcroft, Mary Chadwick, Mrs Muriel Clayton, Mrs Caroline Clegg, Philip Dunne, Bryan Fennell, Peter Fisher, Harry Francis, Andrea Goffee, Doreen Hacking, John Hargreaves, Keith Hayhurst and Lancashire County Cricket Club, Jim Holt, Michael Holt (Edenfield), Stanley Hoyle, David Knight (Stonyhurst College librarian), Clifford Lewer and members of his family, Stewart and Lynne Longworth, Tom Mills, Gordon Moore, Dennis Nuttall, Kay Ogden, Leslie Pilling, Tony Prince (Preston), Jackie Ramsbottom, Ian Summers, Betty and Joe Taylor (Whitworth), John B. Taylor for a characteristic sketch, Joe Teasdale, Bill Turner and Derek Woodall.

Efforts have been made to trace the owners of copyright photographs and obtain permission to reproduce. If I have unwittingly infringed any copyrights, my humble apologies.

Apologies also for any errors that may have crept in due to personal lack of knowledge. I have tried to be as succinct and accurate as possible, but am aware that I may not always have succeeded. The age of infallibility has yet to dawn!

To those who have loaned pictures or shared memories – I am grateful to you all.

Ken Bowden, February 2002

The Committee of the
ST JOHN
Ambulance Brigade
Fern Hill & Acre Mill
Aux.ry Military Hospitals, Bacup

desires to offer this token of remembrance and appreciation to

Ethel Holt

in recognition of valuable services rendered on behalf of the sick and wounded during the Great War, 1914-1919.

1914 · 1919

President & Treasurer.

Medical Officers

Clara A. Shepherd for Committee.

Bacup, January 1920.

Commanding Officer.

"There is one thing without which human life becomes a burden that is, human sympathy."

"He serves most who serves his country best"

Illuminated by ALAN TABOR, Manchester.

Several notable Rossendale buildings were requisitioned for use as military hospitals during the First World War, including Newhallhey House in Rawtenstall (see page 77), the Public Hall at Haslingden and Fern Hill House in Stacksteads. Three Bacup doctors were the divisional surgeons for the St John's Ambulance Brigade, and at the end of hostilities certificates such as this were issued to the cheerful volunteer staff. There used to be four St John's Ambulance divisions in Rossendale, based at Bacup, Haslingden, Rawtenstall and Crawshawbooth. All have now ceased to operate, though several individuals continue the work for which 'St John's' is renowned.

One
Whitworth and its Valley

'If you've any *Whitworth* having, you'd better *Shawforth* and *Facit*'

Five views of Whitworth dating from the 1930s. Riddihough Court and Masseycroft elderly peoples' dwellings are now on the site of the former station; Lloyd Street shows the former allotments and has since been built up – the view is taken from the Orama Mill side looking up the Whitworth Valley; Market Street is basically unchanged; Whitworth Church School was demolished during the 1940s. The 'new steps' are at the end of Hallfold.

Vincent Raymond Clegg (1928-1996), affectionately regarded as 'Mr Whitworth', devoted his life to his native village. The last chairman of Whitworth Urban District Council (1973-74), and the first mayor of the new Parish Council (1974-75), he was the first councillor from Whitworth to be mayor of Rossendale (1986-7) and in 1993 was elected mayor of Whitworth yet again. A man 'not easily gagged', he was an ebullient character never afraid of controversy, who brought a loud voice of common sense to many a council debate.

Healey Dell, a picturesque corner of the present borough of Rossendale, was developed with walkways in the 1920s, the approximate date of this picture. Towering 105ft above the Dell is a viaduct of eight stone arches, each spanning 30ft, built between 1865 and 1870 by the Lancashire & Yorkshire Railway Company to carry trains across the valley. It now carries a sewer from Whitworth to Rochdale. (In the bottom of the dell can be seen 't'owd mill i' t' Thrutch', rumoured to date from Anglo-Saxon times. In this fulling mill, the cloth was impregnated with lant (stale urine) trampled into the cloth).

Sergeant Mathew Bradshaw Butler, England's biggest policeman, was 6ft and 1 inch tall, and born at Pilling on 16 March 1862. After early experience as a tailor with R.S. Benson at Pilling, he was initially appointed to the police force the week after his twenty-first birthday, being posted initially at Accrington, then shortly after his marriage to a Freckleton lady, was posted to Rochdale in October 1884 for the 'Good of the Service', where he spent the rest of his career. Promoted to Sergeant on 1 March 1898, he spent ten years in Whitworth, (where 'on account of his large stature, Mr Butler attracted much attention: at one time he was the tallest and heaviest sergeant in England performing police duty'.) It is believed that the 'good of the service' postings were light duties because of the rheumatic state of his feet. He was eventually pensioned off on 1 April 1909, with a pension of £68 18s 0d per annum, and retired to Kirkham, where he died on 26 September 1911 at the age of forty-nine.

Panoramic view of Whitworth as seen from Hallfold, c. 1920. St Bartholomew's church is just right of centre, and Hallfold Lodge is at bottom right. Also visible is Thorcroft, the home of the Thorburn family, who were descended from one of Hallfold Congregational church's best-loved pastors, Revd William Reid Thorburn (1806-1875 and pastor of Hallfold 1834-1847), whose home 'radiated a particularly sweet and saintly influence throughout the district'.

The tower of St Bartholomew's church, Whitworth, showing several of the character-filled gargoyles which remain a distinguishing feature. The first reference to St Bartholomew's church is in 1529, though the present building dates from 1847. This building is in the Gothic style of architecture, appropriately restored after a major fire in 1984.

General view of Facit from just below the level crossing, looking up Station Road towards Halfway House. Note the railway line in the foreground, with the weaving shed belonging to Spodden Mill in the centre (and chimney on the right), Facit (New) Mill which is still there, and Brown Wardle in the background.

12

Exterior and interior of Facit Wesleyan chapel c. 1910. Originally built in 1851, the chapel was enlarged in 1867 and schools added behind at a total cost of £2,793. Member Joshua Hoyle, (1874-1937) was accepted for the itinerant Wesleyan ministry, serving as a missionary to Burma, followed by pastorates in England and Wales. Centenary celebrations were held in October 1952 but final services took place not many years afterwards on 27 August 1961. The church was demolished shortly afterwards and four modern houses built on the site. The bridleway on the right of the exterior view linked on to Limersgate via 'Upwood' (Hopwood Barn Farm).

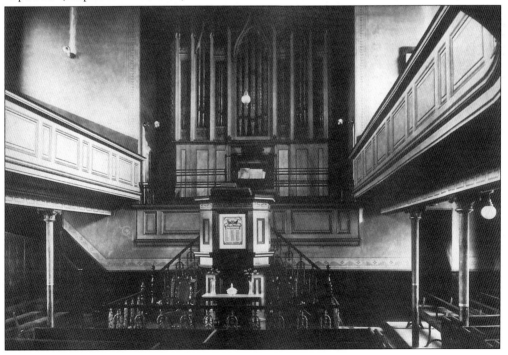

The level crossing on Tong Lane, Facit, showing railway engine 43903 travelling towards Rochdale. The signal cabin was on the down side of the line and the crossing keeper's cottage on the up side. One chuckles at the thought that the toilet was on the opposite side of the railway line from the crossing keeper's house.

St John's church and school, Facit, 3 July 1948. Note the railway in the foreground, unused for passenger traffic, but still open for goods at the time. A Rochdale Corporation bus is en route to Bacup. Barlow Bottoms is at bottom left, approach to the site of which is now blocked by large boulders by the main road. Behind the church stands High Barn (Lane) Farm.

'Summit Cottages', Shawforth. During the royal visit to Rossendale, 9 July 1913, King George V and Queen Mary called at no. 43 (the fourth house along) for afternoon tea. While Queen Mary was upstairs, the King asked if weaver William Ford, took any holidays. 'Yes, St Annes at Whitsuntide'. The royal response was, 'I was at St Annes yesterday…it is a beautiful place'. Did the King know that a Rossendale syndicate had been responsible for the rise of St Annes nearly forty years earlier?

John Head (1851-1919) was connected with the Sugden pharmaceutical line by marriage, and was for forty-five years a staunch supporter of Facit Wesleyan chapel. A man of cautious and sound judgement and unfailing courtesy, his principal shop was at 77 Market Street, Shawforth, though he later opened another branch shop at 465 Market Street, Whitworth. The advert above dates from 1923. He made the celebrated Whitworth Red Bottle, a legacy of the famous and unorthodox Whitworth Doctors.

Shawforth Wesleyan Sunday School, 1923, perhaps on the occasion of the Good Friday walk. From left to right, back row: Tommy Maden, Walter Harrison, Clare Brown, Walter Sidebottom (Superintendent), Revd Thomas Turnbull (Minister 1922-25), Jane Entwistle, Jack Butterworth, Stanley Mellor, Arthur Fielding. Middle row: Ida Kershaw, ? Tattersall, Winifred Wallace, Phyllis Coppin, Clarice Coppin, Rene Hardcastle, Clara Sanderson, Maggie Ashworth, Gwennie Bower, Mary Stott, -?-, Susan Clegg, Annie Mills, Emily Greenwood. Front row: Elsie Lord, Martha Tattersall, Alice Stenhouse, Margaret Shaw, Edith Kershaw, Una Kershaw, Greta Mellor, -?-, Edith Jackson, -?-, Ethel Glue.

Beulah Methodist chapel after destruction by fire in October 1892. Beulah originally began in 1851, and the chapel reopened July 1894 after the fire. The cost of rebuilding was £1,367 15s 0d. The congregation eventually quit this building in July 2000. In September 1892, the attention of Bacup Watch Committee was drawn to the total inadequacy of fire appliances, but no action was taken until after the Beulah fire, when, of the six lengths of hose available, five had burst! One length of hose and one stand pipe were all that remained. By the end of 1892 a hose cart, 180 yards of hose and a further stand pipe were acquired and in May 1894 the Bacup Borough fire brigade were officially established with a new horse-drawn Merryweather steam fire pump.

Two

Bacup

'Bacup is reputed by some to be the last place that God made – and forgot to finish.'

General view of Bacup. The environs of Stubbylee have not changed greatly. Stubbylee Hall (once the residence of James Maden Holt and subsequently the seat of Bacup Borough Council operations) is still in use as the engineering and planning department of Rossendale Council. Bacup cricket field, at 920ft above sea level, is the highest ground in the Lancashire League. What from 1939 to 1985 was Blackthorn Secondary School is now Thorn School.

Aerial view of Bacup, from over Bankside, June 1925. The white house in the left foreground is High Meadows, and St Mary's Catholic church is at the left-hand edge. South Street runs straight up from the bottom where even-numbered properties on St James Street have recently been demolished in front of the Conservative Club and Irwell Terrace chapel. Behind the Co-op building and the baths in the centre can be seen the 'Co-houses' and their allotments, also Central Schools, occupied by pupils of Thorn until 1986. Mettle Cote Farm is behind. In front and to the left of the Co-op and the baths is the Club House property, including the Temple Court area, once full of back-to-back houses and crammed with over 300 people.

Mettle Cote Farm, with its 1751 datestone on the lintel, was demolished to make way for the post-war Fairview estate. Pictured above, around 1900 are members of the Barlow farm family: Annie and Bertha (the children), faced by Ernest Edward Barlow and his wife Alice (Grandad and Grandma) with Gyp the dog in front.

This picture by Edwin P. Morris was passed by the censor and appeared with the caption, 'Bomb Crater in Roadway with Damaged Houses in Background'. The overall headline in the *Bacup Times* read: Damage by Nazi bombers in a north-west town, October 1940. No specific details were given at the time, it would never have done to give away any information potentially helpful to an enemy! These two houses on Thorn Bank were the only Bacup casualties of the Second World War. Bacup War Savings Committee were quick to use this picture as a propaganda exercise urging support for War Weapons Week the following May on the grounds that the residents had nothing with which to respond to the invaders!

The Britannia Coconut Dancers of Bacup, formed 1903, pictured here in the early 1970s. Every Easter Saturday the team meet at the Travellers' Rest on the Bacup/Whitworth boundary at 9 a.m. and dance a total of 65 miles within the old Bacup borough boundaries, ending up at the Glen. Their principal dances are the Garland Dance (five different varieties) plus two Nut Dances; 'th'owd Crash' and 'the Figures'. The Garland Dances are spring ritual dances connected with the renewal of crops. The (Coco)Nut Dance is peculiar to the Britannia troupe, the 'nuts' of maple wood being attached to the dancers' hands, knees and belts. From left to right, back row: Billy Shufflebottom, Alan Edwards, Dick Shufflebottom, Dave Smith, John Flynn (leader), Derek Pilling. Front row: Frank Simpson, Philip Furlong, Brian Daley, John Daley.

Bacup Cricket Club: The Authorised History, published two years ago and still on sale was the catalyst for greater achievements. The team, inspired by Australian professional Adam Dale, won the Lancashire League championship in 2000 with 218 points out of 26 matches played. In 2001 with new professional Shaun Young (Tasmania), they pipped East Lancashire to the title by a mere four points, 244 for 21 wins out of 26 games played. Pictured is the 2001 team squad. From left to right, back row: Alick Ormerod (manager), David Ormerod, Matt O'Connor, John Chapman (stumper with 49 victims), Terry Lord, Dominic Ayres, James Cunliffe, Andrew Spencer, Ruth Syers (scorer). Front row: Peter Thompson, Tim Farragher, Shaun Young, Neal Wilkinson (captain), Peter Killelea, David Thompson.

The small pool at Bacup Baths. This was officially the second-class swimming baths, where several of Bacup's proficient swimmers learned, among them David Billington, Madge Marlow and Joshua Chatburn. Standing at the edge of the baths is baths superintendent Syd Mustow (in charge 1920-1949), curiously he was unable to swim himself!

It is many years since Willie Foster (1890-1963) was the youngest member of the 4x200m freestyle quartet which won Olympic gold medals in London in 1908, following this achievement with bronze medals four years later in Stockholm. Foster was also Bacup Borough swimming champion for 17 consecutive years, 1906-1922. However, much more recently, a Stacksteads visitor to the USA (pictured, right) became an unofficial extra bearer of the Olympic torch as it was carried though Boston in July 1996 prior to its arrival in Atlanta, where Mohammed Ali lit the Olympic flame to herald the Centennial Games.

St James Street, Bacup, showing even-numbered properties on the banks of the river Irwell. These properties were demolished early in 1925. Some shops can be matched with their owners. At no. 2 (the end nearest the Mechanics/Library) was William Glasgow, the furniture broker; at no. 8 was J.T. Cockrill, hatter (see advert below); at no. 10 was Frank Harrison's barber's shop with pole just visible, while the British Legion Club was at no. 12 in the tallest building on the row. No. 20 – at the end – was John 'Tinner' Taylor's ironmonger's. Behind can be seen Irwell Terrace Baptist chapel, the top of the three-storeyed Conservative Club and Tong Mill chimney.

Mark Cockrill (1848-1900) celebrated his coming of age by setting up in business on the banks of the river Irwell at 8 St James Street, in addition taking his father-in-law into partnership as Coops & Cockrill at Rossendale House (over the road at no. 11), where he specialized in tailoring. He was also organist and choirmaster at Waterside Methodist Church for over fourteen years. His son John Thomas Cockrill qualified as a master tailor in 1897 and continued the business after his father's death in July 1900. He too was organist and choirmaster at Waterside until he left the area for health reasons, and died at Blackpool in October 1950 at the age of seventy-six.

Bacup's premier hostelry seen from the Yorkshire Street side. Notice Young J. Ashworth's greengrocers stall on the extreme left. Parts of the George & Dragon dated from the sixteenth century. It was the venue for meetings of magistrates and on the Bridge Street side was the terminus for horse-drawn buses from Rochdale. It lost its licence in May 1909 and was demolished as part of the Townhead clearance scheme during 1925.

Town Head, Bacup in 1927, after the demolition of the old Townhead property, the George & Dragon and the seven shops that filled the space now occupied by the traffic island in St James Square. Notice the tram cables – trams operated from 1911 to 1932 on the Rochdale route.

Ross Mill at night, illuminated like an ocean liner and visible for many miles around. Building of the mill commenced in 1907, but this monument of Edwardian splendour was too late to be protected by any preservation order, so the mill was demolished in 1981, soon after closure, with the chimney the last part to be felled in October 1982.

Nineteen years after his father had visited Rossendale en route from Cornwall to Aberdeen, General Bramwell Booth of the Salvation Army visited Bacup on 15 September 1923 during the course of a ten-day tour of the north west. His 'Reception and Wayside' meeting was in Lee Street at 4 p.m., not far from the army's original 'barracks' at the former Atlas Works in Henrietta Street. The army's first home in Bacup was on Burnley Road, opened May 1886. The *War Cry* of 30 October 1886 reported the conversion of Happy Jane. Ormerod Haigh, later steward of Weir Liberal Club, was for over forty years Colour Sergeant for the Salvation Army in Bacup. The army regularly held open-air meetings at the bottom of Bankside, and during their sixty-year history had premises in Burnley Road, Market Street and finally in South Street, where the Bacup corps closed on 4 February 1947. The whereabouts of the Bacup Salvation Army history book is unknown.

Benjamin Thomas, a native of Cleckheaton, had his likeness painted in April 1845 by Alnwick artist J. Wood. Benny Mark's father was, for many years prior to 1840, the only letter carrier in Bacup, being paid a penny for each letter delivered, the accumulation of which was reckoned as his wages. Benny followed in his footsteps in the early 1840s. Bacup's first postman, Benny Mark was a cordwainer in addition and at one time was also the local bellman. An enthusiastic worshipper at Mount Pleasant Wesleyans, he often shouted out 'Hallelujah!' or 'Glory!' He died in April 1875 at the age of seventy.

In 1922 a teenager guiding his Baptist minister round Kilnholme Mill was advised: 'Why not work to build a new factory under modern conditions?' The youth was local entrepreneur John Willie Johnson. In 1976 his firm, E. Sutton & Sons, expanded into the only purpose-built footwear factory in Bacup, at Riverside, on the site of India Mill and the railway station. Ten years later, chairman J.W. Johnson showed his personal appreciation of services rendered by his employees by giving every single one of his employees a personal bonus gift of £80 on reaching his eightieth birthday. The picture marked forty years of production in Bacup. Left to right, back row: Bob Uttley, Gilbert Maden, Harry Francis, Eric Whitaker, Alan Jackson, Vincent Clegg (mayor), John W. Johnson, Jack Francis, Len Gregson (bank manager), Tom Martin, Leslie Clegg. Front row: Anne Clegg, David Trippier MP, Gladys Witham, Mrs Caroline Clegg (mayoress).

William John Tyne came from Barnsley to acquire the general printing and stationery business from Thomas Brown (who in April 1865 had originated the *Bacup Times*) in 1869, first at no. 7 Market Street, and then from 1877 at no. 23. From these premises he published the Wesleyan Methodist weekly evangelical newspaper *Joyful News*, first issued 22 February 1883. In 1890 Tyne moved to Stockport, where he continued publishing *Joyful News*. Rossendale Stationery & Printing Works, having become Tyne & Shepherd, subsequently became Shepherd, Swire & Markham, and from 1916 Shepherd & Markham, until on the retirement of the owner on 3 April 1993, the shop closed.

Advertisement from the 1930s.

JOYFUL NEWS.

A Journal devoted to Recording and Spreading the Glad Tidings of Salvation.

EDITED BY REV. THOMAS CHAMPNESS.

| o. 1. | Registered for Transmission Abroad. | THURSDAY, FEBRUARY 22, 1883. | Price ONE HALFPENNY. |

Joyful News masthead. This was Methodism's first illustrated weekly newspaper, and ran until the end of 1963, though its first publisher (and the paper) left Bacup in 1890. The 'Hints' are still mainly pertinent! 'Hints to those who write for this paper 1. Be interesting 2. Never use two words when one will do 3. Do not exaggerate 4. Write on one side of the paper only 5. If you are not an educated person do not worry about grammar or spelling, we will make it all right 6. Sign your name, and send it to Rev. T. Champness, 80, Bradford Street, Bolton'.

HE BACUP CHRONICLE,

AND ROSSENDALE ADVERTISER.

PUBLISHED ON THE FIRST SATURDAY IN EVERY MONTH.

| 6.] | JULY, 1855. | [PRICE ONE PENNY |

Masthead of the *Bacup Chronicle*, the first newspaper to be issued in Rossendale, initially on the third Saturday of January 1855, but soon advanced to the first Saturday in the month. Only three copies are known to exist, and even the British (Museum) Library do not have any copies. It was published by John Bentley, stationer, of Yorkshire Street, who was sued for libel by St John's Parochial Church Council, and went bankrupt. He died aged sixty-six in May 1887.

27

Bacup railway station in the early years of the twentieth century, showing a period
advertisement and two platforms looking towards Stacksteads. The buildings on the right of the
railway line are now the site of Sutton's Riverside works. Note the different means of
illumination: the gas lamp on the left, and the older naptha lighting on the right.

Evacuees arriving at Bacup station at the beginning of September 1939. They were taken by bus
to various reception centres, where they were allocated to their hosts in different parts of Bacup.
One adult helper was assigned to every ten children. Note across the road some of the multi-
storeyed Market Street property on the Plantation Street side.

Abraham Dewhurst was a well known Bacup character whose sobriquet was 'Mad Ab'.

He had several different jobs, but his eccentricity was attributed to his being the victim of unrequited love. He was usually seen thereafter wandering the streets chewing his coat collar or a piece of sacking. He sold oatcakes, by courtesy of his friend Mr Farrar, inviting potential customers to serve themselves from his large clothes basket. He also went from door to door hawking milk, and afterwards would wash his container out in the not so clean waters of the River Irwell. He was reported to have considerable savings and investments, but died on 2 October 1892 at Haslington Union Workhouse and was buried at Cross Stones, Todmorden.

Richard Taylor's normal occupation was that of master spindle maker at Underbank Mill, and he was therefore known as Spindle Dick. When the cotton trade was going through a bad spell in the 1860s, he took on an extra job, that of Ale-Taster, an appointment made by the Halmot Court. His badge of office was a pewter gill measure embossed with the seal of the Court. He held the position for seven years without any official remuneration. To him good beer was Allsops, bad beer was Allslops and ginger beer was Allpops. He died 10 October 1876, leaving a son, John Gentleman Taylor – so named because his father was determined to have at least one gentleman in the family.

Northern School during the First World War boasted several scholars who were never absent during the years recorded on their slates. Three of them did not miss a single day's school for five consecutive years or more. From left to right, back row: James Chaffer, Jack Wilkinson, John Willie Johnson, Jennie Whalley, Florrie Hargreaves. Front row: Ernest Law, Ivy Whalley, Hilda E. Johnson, Leonard Johnson, Sarah G. Johnson, Alice Southern.

Deerplay Inn, pictured a century ago, is reputed to be the fourth highest public house in England at 1,324ft above sea-level. It was originally on the opposite side of the road (and therefore within the official Bacup boundary, which the present inn is not!) when its name was the Stag and Hounds.

Panaoramic view of Weir, seen from the Heald Town side in the 1930s. The Irwell Springs premises are seen behind the second of the two lodges which are still there. The mill chimney is belching out its smoke. Wesley Terrace is in the middle, and the former Heald chapel (now Deerplay Rest Home) just above. Recent housing developments have changed the face of Weir considerably.

The source of the river Irwell comprises two streams which rise in the fields of Irwell House Farm (Chadwicks) a few hundred yards behind the Deerplay Inn, and officially beyond the Rossendale boundary in Cliviger.

The first military funeral of the First World War in Bacup, that of Private Fred Riding (2nd Battalion of the East Lancashire Regiment) who died of war wounds on 20 May 1915. Visible on the left is Marks & Spencer's Penny Bazaar, which operated at 8 Bridge Street from 1914 to the end of 1920. That shop, along with others occupying the area where St James Square currently stands, was demolished in the Townhead clearance scheme of 1925.

The Bacup branch of the British Legion was initially at 12 St James Street, but in 1929 new premises were opened behind Bacup station, as seen in 1932. From left to right, back row: T. Hereward, J. Gilbert, H. Hayhurst, W. Evans, R. Amyes, S. Wright, A. Crabtree, L. Slattery, J.W. Hoyle, W. Haigh, W.J. Hargreaves, R.H. Etherington. Middle row: J. Walsh, H. Casson, J.H. Coupe, E.W. Sturt, J.A. Stocks (President), R. Ager, D. Warren, C.H. Barker. Front row: J. Jackson, A. Seville, J.R. Crankshaw, J. Clayburn, H. Laycock, H. Lane, S. Loach, J.R. Ashworth. The British Legion club closed at the end of October 1997, mainly due to the age of current members and the apparent lack of interest by younger people.

Sharneyford School. Most of the class of 1939 pictured at the fiftieth anniversary reunion on 14 September 1989. From left to right, back row: Jack Nuttall, Denis Lord, Neal Nuttall, Leslie Walters, Alan Hirst, Clarence Sanderson, Jim Aspden, Eric Mitchell, Derek Edwards, Roy Halsall, Ralph Thomas, Alfred Hiam. Second row from back: Bertha Gorton (*née* Beeby), Edith Lord, Eveline Lord (*née* Mitton), Muriel Dixon (*née* Sanderson), Brenda Hargreaves (*née* Whittam), Muriel Wright (*née* Dobson), Geoffrey Davison, Gladys Heyworth (*née* Walters), Derek Ford, Harry Cain, Edith Cross (*née* Whitworth), Peter Ford, Neville Ford, Rachel Kenyon (*née* Ashworth), Granville Thomas, Duncan Whittam. Second row from front: Doreen Dawson (*née* Pickup), Patricia Sandham (*née* Nuttall), Hilda Hollingsworth (*née* Mitchell), Marjorie Shorrock (*née* Thornhill), Betty Guest (*née* Whittaker), Anne Clarke (*née* Sanderson), Enslin Stevenson (*née* Jackson), Doreen Earnshaw (*née* McManus), Jean Dunn (*née* Morley), Edith Taylor (*née* Taylor). Front row: Jack Francis, Joan Darwen (*née* Aspden), Florence Jenkins (*née* Hurrell), Leslie Davison.

Sharneyford old chapel, 1851. The Wesleyan Methodists at Sharneyford worshipped here for twenty-five years or so, when for reasons so far undiscovered, they left these premises to worship in the day school lower down the road for a further 125 years until the society ceased in June 2001. Occupied as a garage for Hargreaves' Collieries Company steam wagons from 1914 until the late 1920s, the building was transformed a few years ago into a private residence named Capella House.

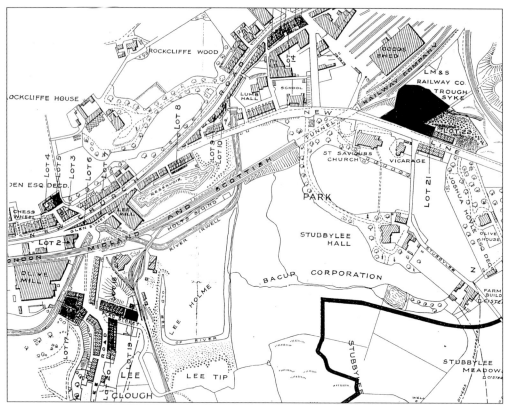

Map of Lee Mill, dated 1927, showing Chess Wheel, an intriguing name which may be where weavers' cottages existed atop a chessel (cheese vat). Part of the Fernhill estate, and at the ward boundary, Chess Wheel was home to three families in 1841, four in 1851 and in 1861 had eight addresses, of which one was a stable and another a shippon. The first internment at St Saviour's was a quarryman from here.

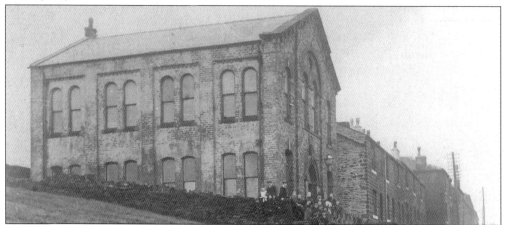

Change Primitive Methodist chapel, built in 1872 to accommodate a congregation which had outgrown the small room where the cause began in 1857. It lasted until 1919, after which the premises were demolished, reusing much of its stone in the erection of nos 1 and 2 Chapel Villas on the site. It was the home of Change Brass Band, who on Band Sunday each November used to take part in the afternoon service.

34

Three
Stacksteads and Wolfenden Areas

'Stacksteads...a valley-bottom roadside settlement.'

Greeting card of Stacksteads from the 1920s. The station is no longer there, Fearns Moss has acquired a school on the left-hand side, Greens Lane remains in somewhat sylvan splendour beyond Springhill, and Newchurch Road no longer has visible tramlines.

Brunswick Terrace, still there today but shown here about a century ago. Bacup Cemetery is around the corner at the top. Every time the rent man called, the lady of the house would warn her neighbour by knocking on the back of her fireplace with the poker. This happened all the way down the row, and so the rent man would go away unrewarded, as everyone pretended not to be in. Consequently, the terrace was always known as *Poker Row*.

Acre Mill Baptist church walking day, *c.* 1912. The middle of the three men at the front is Ernest Kinsella, for whom organist R.H. Ashworth dedicated and named a hymn tune after his friend's safe return from the Boer War. In the distance can be seen the hoarding at the bottom of Huttock End Lane, and the procession is on the Bacup side of the Toll Bar.

Barcroft's grocers shop at 248 Newchurch Road, April 1952. The shop opened in 1907 at 258 Salem Terrace and closed in November 1968. Pictured, from left to right, are: Ernest Barcroft (thirty-six years a member of Bacup Council and mayor from 1944-46), together with his staff Denis Moore, Alan Taylor, Leslie Pearson, Annie Taylor (later Dawson, *née* Barcroft), and John Bartle Stott.

Mr and Mrs John Bartle Stott of Stacksteads. The son of Bacup policeman Tommy Stott, John B. Stott was employed for fifty years at Barcroft's (see above). He married Elizabeth Ellen Tattersall at Zion Baptist church on 18 February 1928 and when he died, on 17 July 1999, they had been married for 71 years and 149 days. Were they the longest-married couple in Rossendale?

Stacksteads Toll Bar in the late 1930s, showing Duckworth's shop (which opened on 18 March 1926) and the first local Belisha crossing, named after Lord Hore-Belisha, who during his period as Minister of Transport (1934-37) introduced the beacons to mark pedestrian crossings.

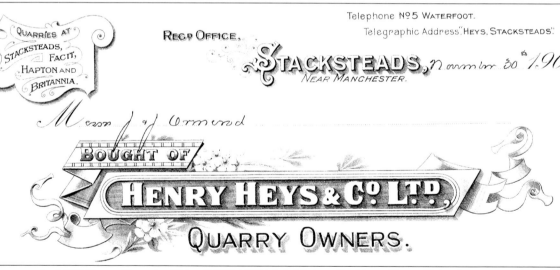

In 1848 Henry Heys the Elder (1815-1889) left Higher Cockham Farm, Helmshore, to try his hand at getting stone that others had considered too difficult to excavate. He eventually developed the stone-quarrying business in Rossendale beyond expectations, and at its peak in 1928, Henry Heys' quarries at Britannia were producing 100,000 tons of stone a year, reputedly the largest freestone quarry in the British Isles. His ornate letterhead confirms where his other quarries were, at Facit (Hall Cowm), Stacksteads (Rakehead), and Hapton (between Burnley and Accrington).

Barnsley Football Club have only won the FA Cup once. This was in 1912 and the team, all but one of them colliers, wore boots made by Harold Crawshaw, a native of Waterbarn, who after serving his apprenticeship locally had set up on his own account at Stairfoot, Barnsley, as a clogmaker and pit boot maker. An active sportsmen himself, he played football for Cloughfold Albion reserves, until an opposing goalkeeper kicked his feet from under him necessitating eventual amputation of his left leg in September 1939. Returning to Rossendale as a semi-invalid, he set up shop at 416 Newchurch Road, where he supplied handmade clogs to the film company which made the 1950s comedy film *Hobson's Choice*. In July 1958 he celebrated his golden wedding, but died on 22 November 1958 at the age of seventy-one.

The grocery business at 462 Tunstead Mill existed for well over 100 years from J.E. Hamer, advertising in 1887 as the 'People's Grocer', until the business was bought by James Crabtree in 1922. It remained in the Crabtree family for seventy-one years until Arthur Crabtree's enforced retirement after an accident in 1993. He always reckoned that his was the only remaining *family* grocer between Bacup and Rawtenstall. This advertisement dates from 1892.

'The Glen', as the Thrutch Gorge is known, is 120ft deep. It is believed to have been formed by the river Irwell during the Ice Age when its original course was blocked by ice. Here, road, river and rail are in close proximity, and in this picture by Harry Firth around 1912, a steam train is seen emerging from one of the three railway tunnels at Waterfoot at the same time as a train enters the Glen from the Bacup end. On the far right is the former Baxter's Brewery and its 192ft-high chimney known as 'Old Smokey', erected to that height to avoid the peculiar air currents in the Glen.

James Brown belonged to the Grant clan of Craigellachie, a prominent hill above the valley of the Strathspey in the Scottish Highlands. Their battle-cry was 'Stand fast, Craigellachie!' Known as 'Scotch Jimmy' or 'The Mayor of Stacksteads', his local notoriety stems from a dispute with the Poor Law Guardians which began in 1877 and dragged on for years. Then on 26 April 1884 occurred his 'grotesque fanfaronade' when he rode his piebald charger into Bacup and declared the new bridge (at the bottom of South Street over the Irwell) formally open. For the occasion he wore a scarlet cloak, a 'fore-and-aft' cocked hat surmounted by Prince of Wales's plumes, a brass 'mayoral' chain and badge, and over his shoulder a huge claymore which he maintained had done service in the defence of Bonnie Prince Charlie at the battle of Culloden (see *A Second Bacup Miscellany*, (1975) pp 63-68).

Waterfoot centre, decorated to mark Queen Victoria's Golden Jubilee in 1897. On the left, Trickett's Arcade had still to be built. Even Dental Villa, a familiar landmark since 1898, had still to be erected.

Myrtle Grove Mill, built in 1854 by Edward Rostron for felt-making purposes and shown here welcoming Prime Minister Lord Salisbury, whose principal engagement was the opening of Waterfoot Conservative Club in December 1890, followed by an evening meeting at Rowland Rawlinson's new extension to Myrtle Grove Mill. Myrtle Grove Football Club were the forerunners of Rossendale United FC. The mill was demolished in 1982.

Sir Henry Trickett envisaged Waterfoot as the shopping centre of Rossendale, and his brainchild was built on the site previously occupied by the Newmarket, and opened 11 March 1899. Built from the designs of Samuel Thomas Williams, architect, the arcade was one of the first buildings in Rossendale to be equipped with electric light, and comprised twenty-three single and double shops, half of them with living accommodation *in situ*. Note Waterfoot's 'Big Lamp' in the centre.

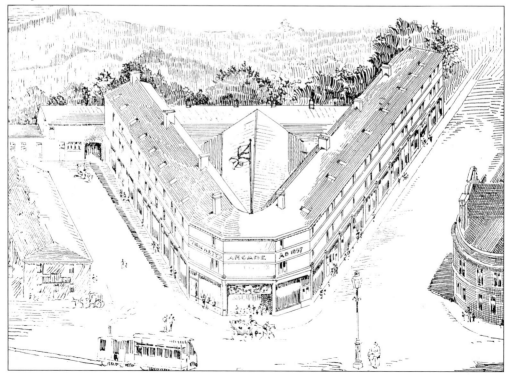

LEWIS NUTTALL

Jeweller and Optician,

SPECIALIZES FOR :: BEST VALUE :: in Engagement Rings and Wedding Rings.

SPECIAL STOCK FOR ALL KINDS OF PRESENTATIONS.

All Repairs executed on the premises. Satisfaction given.

SIGHT TESTING.

Our Scientific Methods at once reveal any weakness or defect.
We cordially invite you to accept our offer to test your eyesight.
Special Room fitted with all necessary appliances.

18, The Arcade, WATERFOOT

Advertisement for Lewis Nuttall, 1903. Though the man died in 1912, the business he founded was still advertising in the Arcade as late as 1948.

Henry Whittaker Trickett, known the world over as the 'Slipper King', was born 23 July 1856 and married 23 January 1879. He served as mayor of Rawtenstall for five years 1898-1903, was elected Freeman of the Borough on 30 May 1907, and knighted in 1909. He died 3 August 1913. This comic postcard features 'a heterogeneous collection of animals being sucked into a Heath-Robinson looking machine at one end, and being flung out at the other as slippers of all kinds of shapes and sizes.'

UP TO DATE.

Fred Edge in his smithy at Warth, just behind the home he shared with Emma for fifty-one years. His father Arthur started the business in 1910 and Fred began work as a half-timer aged twelve, retiring on his sixty-fifth birthday in December 1964. He was Rossendale's last recognized regular farrier. At his peak he was working through the day from 6 a.m. to 8 p.m. He died 20 February 1976.

Mrs Emma Edge, pictured at her 100th birthday celebrations in Lumb Baptist church. Born at Dean Head Farm, she became one of the Rossendale Valley's best known Christian 'characters' and lived a further two years before she died on 24 November 2000 at the age of 102, having survived husband Fred by nearly 25 years.

The last mayor (1972-74) of the former Borough of Rawtenstall, Joe Connolly's thirty-seven years' continuous public service on Rossendale Council and the old Rawtenstall Borough Council was honoured by his election in June 1994 as Rossendale's first (and, so far, only) Freeman. Here he is pictured with the street named after him on 26 June 1996, which was built on the site of the former Baltic Mill, (demolished in 1993). The fifty-three-property housing complex was built under the auspices of the West Pennine Housing Association.

Bridge End Mill at Waterfoot suffered over £5,000 worth of damage as a result of this fire on 12 January 1911. The mill was actually rebuilt, and was owned by MASCO for several years from 1924, but further fires, coupled with an economic downturn resulted in the mill's final closure in 1952. It was demolished five years later, and the present Waterfoot Health Centre was built on the site.

An area of Waterfoot locally known as 'Little Venice'. There are still half a dozen such footbridges which gave this area its name. The former railway bridge (at the bottom of Cowpe Road) was demolished in the late 1980s.

Cowpe Lench is on the opposite side of the river Irwell from the township of Newchurch. The waterfalls at Lench are still there, virtually unaltered, on the road to Waugh's Well.

Lower Lench Farm, or Roughlee Farm, lies half a mile or so to the west of Greenbridge. Said to have been the site of an old Rochdale diocesan chapel used by monks on the old highway from Rochdale to Colne, it is notable for its cruck roof members, parts of which date from the sixteenth and subsequent centuries. Farmed for many years by the Ashworths, the last Ashworth (George) died 18 January 1970 at the age of seventy-nine, leaving five daughters but no sons. Three of his grandsons are pictured here in 1949: John Dixon, Colin Jackson, and William Abbott.

Cowpe School and Memorial. Opened 13 November to replace earlier premises further up the road at Old Boarsgreave which had been completed in March 1832. One of the first trustees of the new premises was William Lord, teacher and school superintendent at Cowpe for some forty years and the first mayor of the new Borough of Rawtenstall in 1891. Cowpe was originally part of the Parish of Rochdale and the vicar of Waterfoot used to conduct the regular afternoon service at Cowpe Sunday School, the only place of worship in the village.

Cowpe Reservoir at the end of August 1976 with water levels so low that the remains of the former Black Bank Farm can be seen again. Originally completed and opened on 21 July 1910 after nine years in construction, Cowpe Reservoir comprised a dam of three tiers. It eventually passed out of local control in 1963.

The top end of Cowpe Road, looking towards Kearns Mill, in the summer of 1975. Cowpe dyeing and bleaching mill was originally built around 1825, but was inundated by the Cowpe flood of 4 July 1838 and severely damaged by fire in March 1876, which caused £20,000 worth of damage. Rebuilt, the mill has endured a few changes of ownership but it is now usually known as Kearns' Mill after the family that has occupied it for the last seventy years.

48

Waterfoot, viewed from Thrutch Barn (above the Glen), showing the railway and goods yard, c. 1950. Waterfoot station (closed December 1966) can be seen, with St James' church to the right and Bacup Road on the right-hand edge. All the factories pictured have now disappeared.

Inside J.H. Hirst's Whitewell Works at Waterfoot. John Henry Hirst (1863-1922), the son of a monumental mason at Pippin Bank, Bacup, bought the small Hollins Mill in the Shawclough area of Whitewell Bottom when he was twenty-one. His first order was for felt carpet slippers at $4\frac{1}{2}$d per pair. Seven years later he expanded into Whitewell Works (originally built as a cotton weaving shed). This scene from the closing room was recorded around 1934, with a line shaft running the length of the room, where the upper part of the slipper was stitched together before going on to the lasting room.

S. SUGDEN,
(A. P. S.,)

Family & Dispensing Chemist,

AND SURGEON DENTIST,

→:The Rossendale Pharmacies,:←

WATERFOOT AND NEWCHURCH.

THE ROSSENDALE BLOOD CLEANSER.
Cures Scurvy, Ulcers, Scrofula, Pimples on the Face, and all Blood Diseases. *Price 2/- per Bottle.*

HOP TONIC.
Composed of Hops, Dandelion, Gentian, &c. 1/- *and* 1/9 *per Bottle.*

SUGDEN'S UNIVERSAL FRUIT COUGH ELIXIR.
For Coughs, Colds, Asthma, Bronchitis, &c. *Price* 9½d. *and* 13½d. *each Bottle.*

SUGDEN'S UNIVERSAL TONIC STOMACH PILLS.
For Indigestion, Sick Headache, &c. 9½d. & 1s. 1½d. Boxes.

ORANGE QUININE TONIC WINE.
BOTTLES 1s. 3d. and 2s. 3d. EACH.

Feeding Bottles. Night Lights. Food Warmers

THE GLEN BOUQUET.
A Choice Perfume for the Handkerchief and Toilet. In Bottles. 6d. each.

SUGDEN S GLYCERINE JELLY.
For Healing, Preserving and Softening the Skin. Bottles 6d. and 1s. each.

Samuel Edward Sugden (1816-1881) set up in 1837 as a chemist and druggist and fathered several medical and pharmaceutical worthies. His eldest daughter married John Head who settled in Shawforth. Five of his sons trained and qualified as chemists before entering the medical profession as GPs, all but one ending up in London. The exception was Ebenezer, who practised in Rochdale, became a member of Rochdale Council and whose granddaughter Yvonne was to become British skating champion in 1954. Greenfield House was known for many years as the Doctors' House, occupied by the Sugdens from the early 1860s, and traces of its use as a surgery-cum-pharmacy are still visible eighty-five years after they left. Chalked on a beam in the attic the name of S. Sugden can still be deciphered!

View of Piercy, *c.* 1920. St Anne's imposing vicarage stands out near the top, with the school to its left. Near the bottom left corner can be seen Brooks' slipper works. Joe Brooks lived in the large house further up Ashworth Road. The open space between the vicarage and Charles Street is a reminder that a belt of quicksand made it impossible to build in certain areas.

St James' school, Waterfoot, in 1911. The school ran for many years, but closed around the time of the Second World War. Mrs Ashworth (far right) was the teacher of this class, so far unnamed.

St James' church at Waterfoot boasted a total of twenty-one men and women who had all registered between fifteen and twenty-one years regular and punctual attendance at Sunday school, considered quite an extraordinary achievement in 1920. From left to right, front row: Joseph Nuttall, Harriet Lord, George Arthur Dearden, Annie Howarth, Joseph Hodgson, Ann Whittaker, James Wilson. Middle row (standing): Thomas Edward Halstead, Gertie Howarth, Emily Whittaker, Emma Whittaker, Bertha Whittaker, Emma Ratcliffe, Ethel Maude Dearden, James Mottram, James Lord Day. Back row: Arthur Trueman, James Henry Taylor, Hodgson Whittaker, John William Sellers, Isaac Trueman.

Entrance to the caves at the old Scout quarry facing the former tripe works. These underground quarries were prepared as air-raid shelters during 1938. The source of underground walks, one could enter here and emerge at Bonfire Hill in Crawshawbooth, though that route has now been blocked up. It is believed that a cavern under Seat Naze, accessible via these caves, provided a ready supply of spring water to Newchurch a century ago, as well as to Bowness's mineral works at Shawclough.

Thomas Lord, tripe dresser, died in 1953, his trade being continued by his married daughter, Mary Chiswick. Her father's small tripe works changed hands around 1965 and has since 1985 been the lovely little Scout Rest Home, capacity fifteen residents. Sadly, it has recently closed (March 2002).

SCOUT,

Newchurch, _Nov 13_ 18

_41_

_M_

To George Hardman, Dr

SHOEING SMITH and WHEELWRIGHT.

Interest at the rate of 5% will be charged at the expiration of Three Months.

Letterhead from George Hardman, whose family originally owned a wheelwright's business at Hollin Forge, across the road from the Roe Buck. After a family disagreement, George Hardman set up on his own in the 1880s, and his son, George Hardman the younger, continued the business until around 1950 when he retired. He died some years later at the age of eighty-three.

Newchurch Grammar School, at the corner of Bridleway and Turnpike, which was rebuilt in 1830 and again in 1890, and remained in use until the present Bacup & Rawtenstall Grammar School (although not originally known by that name) opened in 1913. Its motto was 'Alere Flammam Litterarum,' meaning 'May the flame of learning burn'. Its last head (Thomas Ernest Jackson) became the first headmaster of Bacup & Rawtenstall Secondary School (since 1928 B.R.G.S.) The former Newchurch Grammar School was, from the end of 1916, used by local Catholics as a chapel and day school until St Peter's new day school was erected, by which time the building pictured was described as 'the worst in Rossendale' – overcrowded and inadequate for late twentieth-century purposes. It was demolished in 1979. Note the barely altered entrance to Newchurch Wesleyan church on the left.

Caleb Shepherd moved into existing mill premises at Sagar Holme in 1872 as a cotton manufacturer and by 1885 had a labour force of 100 who were operating 170 looms with 7,000 weft spindles, the motive power being supplied by a large 225hp beam engine. The last weaving firm in Whitewell Bottom, the mill ceased trading in 1979 and the only parts still standing are the weaving shed and closing room. Shown above is the interior of the hand twisting room around 1912, with Georgie 'Crutch' at the front and Sam Harrison at the back.

Caleb Shepherd letterhead from the 1920s.

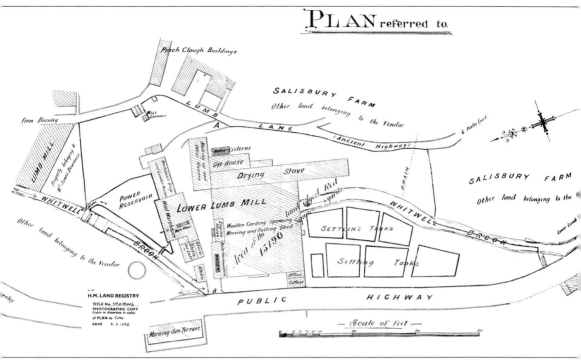

PLAN referred to.

Whitewell Brook (note different spelling here) was one of the main tributaries of the river Irwell. Built adjacent to the river were Lumb Mills, seen in this sketch of 1896, which reveals several interesting features. Lumb Mill was later renamed Higher Lumb Mill, and Lower Lumb Mill renamed Whitewell Vale Mill, the two being linked by gantry.

A more recent picture of the Whitewell Brook at the Hargreaves Arms bend, showing the former St Michael's Vicarage, now Lumb Valley Residential Home for the elderly. Rising at the head of Wolfenden, Whitewell Brook empties itself into the river Irwell below Newchurch.

St Michael's church, Lumb, built 1847-8 in the Norman style on a site donated by John Hargreaves of Blackburn and consecrated 9 December 1848. It closed exactly 153 years later, on 9 December 2001, due to falling numbers and horrendously expensive dry rot repairs. Possibly its most notorious vicar was Revd Theophilus Caleb, whose story is told in *The Rev Theophilus Caleb: Race, Politics and Religion in a South-East Lancashire Village, 1926-1932*, by C.S. Ford (1991).

Revd Theophilus Caleb was born in 1881 in Allahabad, India, son of a Presbyterian minister. Trained as a barrister, he was confirmed as an Anglican in 1902, and served seven curacies in nineteen years before coming to the Lumb Valley. An acerbic personality with High Church principles, he managed to alienate a vast majority of his parishioners, and was eventually inhibited by the Bishop of Manchester from performing his duties, being transferred to Pendlebury, and later to Huttoft in Lincolnshire. The latter church was visited by John Betjeman, who immortalised Caleb in his poem 'A Lincolnshire Church'. Caleb died early in December 1959 at the age of seventy-eight.

Lumb was a good place to be a footballer in the Edwardian era. The village boasted two excellent football teams, Water Albion, who during the 1908-9 season were never defeated, and Water Football Club, who won every game played that season, 29 out of 29, scoring 149 goals in the process, and conceding a mere 12. Not only were they the local league champions, they won the Rossendale Charity Shield and on Good Friday 1909 beat a 'rest of the league' team 1-0. From left to right (excluding man in background), back row: Tom Jeffrey, Ben Gregory, Harry Broxton, Tom Broxton, Dan Holt, Frank Hindle, Sam Maden, Bill Myers. Front row: Jack Gregory, Harry Taylor, Fred Heyworth, Jim Hindle, Ernest Clark, James Broxton.

Dean is a hamlet above Water, famous locally for the boiler explosion of June 1858 which was the subject of the earliest Rossendale photographs extant. Described as the womb of local industry, workers going to the mill from the outlying farms that surround the hamlet would, especially in winter, carry candles in a jar to light their way, like so many fireflies converging on the mill. The demolition of Dean Mill was completed in 1950, and most of the mines which had provided alternate employment in the area soon closed, leaving little but memories. Many of the properties in the area have since been tastefully renovated.

Engraving of Newchurch which appeared in Newbigging's *History of the Forest of Rossendale* and is believed to date from the 1830s. Boothfold is to the right, Seat Naze on the horizon, and the engraving highlights St Nicholas' church and the old school that was later used by the local Unitarians. On the left-hand edge can be seen the footpath known as the Heys, now Church Lane.

Old Street, Newchurch, showing a renovated Lower House. St Peter's presbytery and church are behind. Lower House was from 1820 to 1904 the home of Deborah Ashworth, a local 'character' who never lived anywhere else, then of a family of Scottish footballers. Old Street was always known as Kirk Gate, leading as it does to St Nicholas' parish church. It unfortunately suffered from the municipal vandalism which destroyed much of the character of old Newchurch in the early 1960s, when seventy-two properties were destroyed in the interests of redevelopment.

Aerial view of Newchurch in the early 1920s. At the top can be seen Newchurch Grammar School (by then being used for educational purposes by St Peter's Catholics) and on its left Newchurch Wesleyan church, whose school (and current place of worship) had still to be built (this happened in 1926). The original Mount Tabor United Methodist church can still be seen on the site subsequently occupied by St Peter's. The allotments at the front are now part of the Staghills estate.

Kirk Show 1923. The show that year was held on the Rossendale United football field at Dark Lane. Note St Nicholas' church behind. The Kirk Show went into abeyance after the 1933 show and later attempts to revive it have not proved too successful.

Revd Arthur Gorrill Hopkins (1891-1924) was a scoutmaster supreme, initiating on 3 December 1922 what became known as the Hopkins Own Scout Troop. Awarded the MC in March 1918 for conspicuous bravery in the Gaza-Jerusalem campaign, he was in the first aeroplane to fly over Jerusalem after its capture by General Allenby on 9 December 1917. When visited by two scouts during his last illness, he said: 'I'm going on a long hike soon, and I won't have any pack to carry, and when it rains, you'll know that I kicked St Peter's bucket over!'

Hopkins' Own Scout Troop. The original troop ceased in 1950, but was revived in November 1954 when the founder's son became minister at Newchurch. Sadly this has also ceased to function. The picture shows the first monthly parade service of the revived Troop on 12 December 1954. Left to right, back row: Norman Whitbread, Clifford Green, Peter Isherwood, Robert Jeffrey, Brian Cunliffe, Clifford Lewer, David Whittaker, Geoffrey Colbert, 'Skipper' (Revd W.H. 'Bill' Hopkins). Middle row: Derrick Smith, Frank Pilkington, Barry Taylor, Maldwyn Elmer, Edward Grimshaw, Michael Colbert, David Smith (?), John Harden, John Scholes, Barry Hartley, Bernard Martin, Tony Silvers. Front row: Ian Barratt, Harry Pope, Stephen Whittaker, Stephen Ingham, Roddy Taylor, Gordon Heaton, Glyn Webb. The troop used to enjoy summer camps in different parts of Lancashire, and during the 1939 camp this community song was rendered to the tune of 'Lassie from Lancashire':
'We are Laddies from Lancashire, Jolly good Laddies from Lancashire, 'Ee, its grand to be camping here, 'Ee by Gum… We are camping in Huntroyd Park, Climbing Pendle like mugs in t' dark, Old Mother Demdyke can go on her night hike Wi' t' Laddies from Lancashire…'

Cartoon produced at the Hopkins Own Scout camp 1939 by patrol leader Geoff Colbert, who has been involved with the scout movement virtually all his life.

Newchurch Wesleyan Ladies group, c. 1912. From left to right, back row: Mrs Alice Rothwell, Gertrude Luty, Clara Ingham, Elsie Ingham, -?-. Middle row: Emily Birtwistle (*née* Lee), Sarah Alice Whitehead (*née* Shipley), Margaret Teasdale (*née* Riley), Rhoda Terry, Ellen Riley, Alice Teasdale, Sarah Fielding, Mrs Selina Rothwell. Front row: -?-, Mrs Maggie Baldwin, May Buckley, Myrtle Brennand, Mrs Florence Whitehead, Bertha Shipley (*née* Riley), Ethel Coupe (*née* Luty), Mary Ellen Parkinson (*née* Shipley), Beatrice Whittaker (*née* Terry).

Water Brass Band, founded 1866, is probably the oldest local band still functioning. Pictured on a visit to Southport on Kirk Fair Monday in 1870 are, from left to right: Edmund Pickup, Ormerod Jackson, James Uttley, John Parkinson, Thomas Harrison, Robert Whittaker, William Stansfield, John Jackson, William Parkinson, Robert Hargreaves, Harry Sharp, John Gregory, Isaac White, James Whittaker, Greenwood Hanson, Anthony Dean, James Gregory, John Albert Hargreaves, Frank Nuttall, James Harrison.

Four
Musical Interlude

'Rossendale…a great centre of music, both vocal and instrumental.'

Stacksteads Band dates from at least 1872, and is still going strong 130 years later. For many years they were Stacksteads Prize Band, an appellation earned as a result of winning the Westhoughton Band Contest three years running, 1908-10. Thought to be pictured outside St Joseph's RC church during the 1920s, with conductor Jim 'Bob' Heap (front row, centre), only two members of this band have so far been identified: John Willie Evans (second from left in the back row), and Charlie Evans (third from the left in the middle row).

Founded March 1924, the Rossendale Male Voice Choir published a commemorative seventy-fifth anniversary history (still on sale), detailing its rise from two dozen singers to one of the finest male voice choirs in Britain, winning the Llangollen International Eisteddfod three years on the trot (1952-54) and again in 1958. This previously unpublished picture of the choir is outside Alder Grange High School prior to their visit to Moenchengladbach in September 1994.

Fred Tomlinson was appointed temporary conductor of the newly formed Rossendale Male Voice Choir in 1924. The 'temporary' lasted for over fifty years until he resigned at the age of eighty-three in February 1976. He is pictured after the choir's 'hat-trick' win at Llangollen in 1954.

Rossendale Ladies Choir, at their first rehearsal in January 1977, and still going strong after twenty-five years. They made their TV debut in 1980, joining the Rossendale Male Voice Choir at Preston Guild Hall as guest artistes of the Black Dyke Mills Band. In 1981 they competed for the first time at the Llangollen International Eisteddfod, and the following year made the first of several trips to Bocholt, beginning an enduring link with Rossendale's twin town which has resulted in many lasting friendships. In 1984 they took first place at the Blackpool Festival. Left to right, back row: -?-, -?-, -?-, Bessie Booth, -?-, -?-, Jean Emmett, Lucy Haworth, Alice ?, -?-, Velma Hoyle, Edna Winstanley, Jean Wolfe. Front row: Beatrice Wade (conductor), Barbara Gee, Nellie Hargreaves, Nora McCarthy, June Knight, E. Ashworth, Jennie Newman, Senne Lee, Jean Trickett, Freda Raynor, Kathleen Pickles, Ada Birchall, Doreen Hacking (secretary), Constance Heald (pianist).

Hallfold Congregational church choir, pictured June 1948 after winning the Sir James Duckworth Challenge Cup at the Blackpool Music Festival the previous November. From left to right, back row: J.H. Nuttall, R.C. Stott (later head of Thorn School 1962-72), J. Taylor, A. Whitworth, D.S. Nuttall, J. Rudman, F. Ingham, Jesse Barker, T. Earnshaw, John Barker, T. Hirst. Second row from back: R. Nuttall, Mrs C. Kettleton, Mrs F. Ingham, Miss M. Smith, Mrs H. Hill, Mrs Mercer, Mrs Gowers, Miss E. Rudman (organist), Miss D. Hall, Mrs E. Taylor, Mrs J. Tweedale, Miss M. Palmer, Miss J. Wild. Second row from front: Miss M. Brearley, Miss J. Rudman, Mrs J. Bowers, Mrs I. Taylor, Revd W. Clark, Mr E. Penney (conductor), Mrs R. Nuttall, Mrs W. Rawstron, Miss A.M. Stott, Miss B. Nuttall (later to marry Mr J. Taylor). Front row: C. Proud, Miss J. Collins, Miss E. Nuttall, Miss C. Whatmough, G. Clegg, K. Hoyle.

The Shawforth Drum Majorettes began in 1982 with seven youngsters from that area, increasing within a year to thirty girls aged 8 to 14, and acquiring uniforms, equipment (percussion instruments) and a coach displaying their name. They are pictured here ten years later marching through Carnaby Street for the launch of Virgin Radio on 30 April 1993. Their music, selected from the last fifty years, varies from 'Rock Around The Clock' to 'Bob the Builder'. As ambassadors for the valley they first visited Bocholt in 1988 and several times since, with reciprocal visits from Germany. The Shawforth Drum Majorettes come from all over Rossendale and even beyond, and entertain for charity purposes, with many local fund-raising organisations. Their baton-twirlers and pom-pom girls make an attractive visual impact, and the youngsters pride themselves on a highly disciplined team approach. Enquiries and potential new faces – contact Kay Ogden on 01706-853852.

Theirs was the dream story of a village school choir who entered a nationwide competition and won. Water School Choir took part in a competition organised by McDonalds to celebrate ten years of the Child of Achievement Awards, where they sang the set piece 'That's a Child of Achievement', plus their own choice, 'The Sunny Side of the Street'. Representing the Granada region in the regional finals, Water Choir won at Birmingham in November 1991 and followed this up with a win in the national finals in Cardiff in January 1992. Finally, they won the platinum award for the best choir in the Child of Achievement Music in the Community competition, plus a silver rose bowl as the choir representing England. From left to right, back row: Christopher Phillips, Naomi Bibby, Michael Holland, Edward Matthews, Dee Wild, William Kerr, Jon-Alec Morris, Keely Montgomery, Alex Price, Kate Hartley. Front row: Jemma Taylor, Vicky Eggar, Emily Price, Chrissy Johnson, Donna Uttley, Lisa Bird, Sarah Jordan, Helen Skinner, Jodie Foulds.

The Larks of Dean Quire are spiritual descendants of the original Larks of Dean (or Deighn Layrocks) and revived the group around 1991. The original Deighn Layrocks were a group of amateur church musicians, singers and composers in the Goodshaw area and over the hill around the hamlet of Dean between 1750 and 1850. They were liable to burst into song at any opportunity. The present Quire sing mostly unaccompanied. From left to right, backrow: Diane Sanderson, Chris Gardner, Paul Sanderson, Alan Seymour, Mike Walker, David Stow, Richard France, Steve Tanner, Gill Barnett. Front row: Denise Craven, Ken Craven, Janet MacFarlane, Hazel Walker, Judy Whiting, Jean Seymour. (0161-761-1544 for any enquiries.)

BOCKING WARP. L.M.

Bockings are coarse woollen baize-like fabrics, introduced by the Flemings, and imported by King Henry I. This old ballad popular with the Deighn Layrocks was composed by James Nuttall the elder (1745-1906). The following dialect verse was also sung as an alternative:

Aw think just naah aw see um stand
Wi' candle lifted, book i' hand;
While others on th' owd table spread
Ther book, un pept o'er fiddler's yed.
Then one, two, three, they all began,
Un th' crotchets, quavers, heaw they ran!
Th' owd singers sang, un th' fiddlers bow'd,
Th' effect uth' song con neer be towd.

Whiskey Chorus were formed in 1991. Based in Stacksteads, the trio regularly perform Irish sing-along music. Paul Belger plays banjo, six-string guitar and almost-silent vocals. Ron Suthers provides lead vocals, six- and twelve-string guitars. Peter Barcroft, the longest-staying member of the group, plays bass guitar and mandolin. The name derives from a song of the same title popularized by the Houghton Weavers.

The well-known firm of David Whitehead formed their own band in October 1948. The conductor was Clifton Jones, formerly associated with the Irwell Springs Band. The band eventually folded due to lack of support and the lack of suitable jobs for possible bandsmen to fill. Left to right, back row: A. Wood, W. Seddon, B. Whiteside, H. Hawke, R. White, H. Shaw, J. Gluyas, G. Clarke. Middle row: R. Abbott (librarian), J.H. Huxley, J.B. Hargreaves, J. Barnes, F. Flanagan, A. Nadin, A. Dearden, R. Meadowcroft. Front row: E. Garstang, A. Kay, J. Griffiths (secretary), Clifton Jones (musical director), H. McGrath, W. Butterworth, E. Muldowney.

Founded in 1885, Haslingden Orchestral Society were invited to give a concert at Stonyhurst College's winter Blandyke at the end of January 1894. A Blandyke is a special feast day derived from Blandecques, a locality in the Spanish Netherlands three miles from St Omer, where the oldest Jesuit College in the English-speaking world was founded in 1593, migrating to Stonyhurst in 1794. The visitors' performance was so popular they were invited to return for the 100th celebration at Stonyhurst, the 302nd since the foundation of the original college. They accompanied the procession to Pontifical High Mass on the Tuesday, played 'Rule Britannia' for the centenary dinner next day and also the introductory music for the centenary Operetta. They were so well received that at the end of October 1894 they paid another visit to Stonyhurst. The Orchestral Society continued to entertain until their last concert on 14 November 1934 after a life span of almost fifty years. On that occasion by courtesy of the L.M.S. Railway Company, the train due to leave Haslingden for Manchester at 10.09 was held back for a full five minutes! Standing: J.W. Warburton, J. Haworth, H. Lea, W.H. Weber, J.R. Green, J.L. Byrne, T. Greenwood, E. Whittaker, M. Krauss, J.H. Hughes, C. Simpson, S. Gudgeon. Seated: J. Hough, J. Rishton, T. Warburton, J. Cronshaw, O. Bamber, R. Hoyle, J.S. Green, Revd Fr. Holley.

Alan Rawsthorne, born 2 May 1905, in Haslingden, was the only son of a local GP whose local ancestry dates back over 400 years. The family left for Southport in 1914, and after a brief flirtation with dentistry, Alan entered the Royal College of Music in 1926, and thereafter devoted his life to music, composing *Theme and Variations for Two Violins* (1937), *Symphonic Studies* (1939), *Street Corner Overture* (1944), and *Corteges* (1945). Further symphonies and concertos followed during the 1950s and he was awarded the CBE in 1961. He wrote the Halle overture for the centenary of that orchestra, and also produced a clarinet quartet, three string quartets, film music and the ballet *Madame Chrysantheme*. He died 24 July 1971 in Cambridge at the age of 66, described as one of the major British composers of the twentieth century (picture reproduced by courtesy of the BBC).

Thomas Barnes, renowned as the 'wonderful blind organist' had a capital ear for sounds of any kind. Originally organist at St James' church, Accrington, he was appointed organist at St James' church, Haslingden, in July 1815 at a salary of £12 per annum, plus an annual collection in the church. He lived in Church Lane, where he worked as a handloom weaver. A contributor to the Deighn Layrock tunebooks, he led the procession to the opening of the new Pikelaw Institution, playing 'See the conquering hero comes' on his flute. He died at that same institution aged eighty on 2 October 1874.

Five
Rawtenstall and Points North

'Rawtenstall…a prosperous town which can look forward to the future with confidence.'

Rawtenstall general view. St Mary's church no longer has the tall spire behind the tower, and the mill chimney has long gone. Captain Fold is but a memory, though the former Methodist church in the background has been refurbished as St Mary's Chambers. The entrance to Whitaker Park no longer has its ornate name sign, though the bowling green still functions. Most change is probably evident in Bank Street.

Aerial view of Rawtenstall in the 1920s, with a cricket match in progress top left. Ilex Mill (built 1856) is across the road, and St Mary's church just right of centre. There have been many changes since the '20s.

The Weavers' Cottage, Fallbarn, originally built around 1780 as a loom shop, the top two storeys housing looms and the ground floor being used for finishing purposes. A relic of the days when the cottage textile industry was about to give way to factory production. Note the mullioned windows.

Rescued from possible demolition by Rawtenstall Civic Society, and restored as a Heritage Centre, the top floor boasts a working spinning wheel and handloom, its original fireplace and much of the original ceiling, and the ground floor houses a Victorian kitchen and clog shop. It is open summer weekends from Easter to September.

Where this 2-4-2 tank engine can be seen drawing a train from Rawtenstall up the valley, with a bridge spanning from Hall Carr to the back of Ilex Mill, is now Bocholt Way, and no trace of any railway can any longer be seen at this spot.

The interior of the engine room at Ilex Mill in its heyday. Harry Rayneard was engine tenter and fire beater here for thirty to forty years. Shown is the massive 12ft diameter fly-wheel, weighing 8 tons and carrying 8 ropes each 1½ inches thick. At its peak in 1879 Ilex Mill had 748 looms and 40,000 spindles operating, but changed hands several times before closing in 1981.

The river Irwell at its confluence with the Limy. Longholme Felt Works, owned by Richard Ashworth and later demolished to make way for part of the Asda complex, are on the right. Much of the scene is still visible today, though the signal box and station buildings have gone.

Bury Road, Rawtenstall, looking towards St Mary's church, c. 1950. Longholme Felt Works is on the right. The small roadside building on the right is today an ice-cream parlour, while the railway storage building on the left is now Taylor's car showroom.

Bridge End Cottages, with Longholme Mill behind, stood where Bury Road bends over the river Irwell. Water Street to the left is now the walkway by the side of Asda from the footbridge. Last occupied in 1974, the demolition of these sturdy-looking cottages appears to have been one of the first decisions of the unified Rossendale Borough Council.

During the First World War several local homesteads were requisitioned for use as military hospitals. Newhallhey House, above, considered by some to be of Tudor foundation, but by others to date from the time of Oliver Cromwell, stood near the Haslingden Road end of the site now occupied by the large traffic island. The home of the Nuttall family in the late seventeenth century, its treatment during the First World War hastened its eventual dereliction and demolition to make way for the new bypass in the 1960s.

Jubilee Methodist church, Lord Street, now the site of a new police station. The church opened on 23 June 1861 at a cost of £1,850, with an organ and heating added in 1868 for a further £480. The chapel boasted a minstrel group and even a male voice choir. It closed 3 October 1965 to enable the building of the new police station. Note the railings leading to the rear entrance of the town hall and the modern extension which opened in 1965.

When a prominent Labour MP visited Rawtenstall telephone exchange (upstairs in the post office building in Kay Street) on 3 October 1934, the local press declined to accept this picture, presumably on the grounds that the future Labour Prime Minister was not well enough known! Major Clement Attlee, in the middle of the front row, was Deputy Leader of the Opposition (and Leader from 1935). That evening he spoke at Rawtenstall Library under the auspices of the local Labour Party. Telephone Week in Rawtenstall marked the recent availability of a night telephone service for just one shilling per call. The exchange at Kay Street lasted from 1923 until 1964.

Originally a Toll Bar, Fitzpatrick's herbal health shop is the last temperance bar in Britain. It was established by Malachi Fitzpatrick in 1933. His parents ran similar shops all over Lancashire. A qualified herbalist, he made herbal cures and herbal drinks to unique recipes dating from 1880. Remedies are available for almost every conceivable ailment. He retired in 1982 and died in November 1999 at the age of eighty-eight.

Winston Place, arguably Rossendale's best known sportsman, progressed from his council school team and Cloughfold Wesleyans to his native Rawtenstall's 2nd XI, making his debut at the age of thirteen on 2 June 1928, scoring 15 against Burnley. On 27 July 1929, he made his first team debut, still only fourteen, scoring 7 runs and bowling 3 overs. In 1934 he scored 636 runs for Rawtenstall, including exactly half of the 222 for 2 declared against Ramsbottom at Bacup Road on 9 June, and had a trial at Old Trafford. Next year he topped the Rawtenstall batting averages with 756 runs, and played his first match for Lancashire 2nd XI, scoring 118 runs in 8 innings and being paid £4 10s 0d per match. In his first season on Lancashire Cricket Club ground staff he scored 1,000 runs and made his debut for the County 1st XI in May 1937 with a seventh ball duck at Derby, but in all matches totalled 600 runs. His highest score for Lancashire 2nds was 172 against Durham at South Shields (Durham were all out for 170 in each of their two innings, losing this match by an innings and 31 runs). A chanceless 164 for the County 1st XI against the full might of the West Indies a month later resulted in the award of his county cap. A regular member of Lancashire 1st XI after the Second World War, in 1947 he amassed 2,601 runs, including 266 not out (out of a team total of 512 for 8 declared) against Oxford University in May and a century in each innings of the match against Notts at Old Trafford in August. He shared an unbeaten 1st wicket partnership of 350 with Cyril Washbrook (for whom he was the perfect foil) against Sussex at Old Trafford in May. Chosen to tour the West Indies in 1947-8, he played three Tests, scoring his only Test century (107) at Kingston, Jamaica. He scored over 1,000 runs in eight successive seasons, 1946 to 1953, and took just one 1st class wicket in August 1937, when his bowling analysis read 2 overs for 2 runs and 1 wicket. He retired in 1955 and became a newsagent in Rawtenstall. Unassuming and humble, he was always proud of the fact that his last innings for his country was a century and his last for his town was also a century, 109 not out against Burnley.

Winston Place, born 7 December 1914, died 25 January 2002.

	Matches	Innings	Runs	Average	Catches
Rawtenstall	?	142	2498	20.31	54
Lancashire 2nd	53	80	2158	31.27	36
Lancashire 1st	298	441	14605	36.69	179
Test matches	3	6	144	28.80	0
Other 1st class	23	40	860	21.50	11

Stained glass window in St Mary's recently opened new school at Oakenhead. It incorporates many local details, the holly (Latin *Ilex*, symbol of the Whitehead family), as well as the hills, the Rossendale emblem and the red rose of Lancashire, sun, clouds, rainbow and the river Irwell, besides other school-related items.

Richard Whitaker (1829-1906). Manager at several local cotton mills, including Ilex, he combined great business acumen with a generous compassion for the less fortunate. He always declined public office, though he would have made an excellent mayor. He moved to St Anne's in 1894, but his heart remained in Rossendale and in 1901 he bought the Oak Hill estate and mansion and offered it to Rawtenstall Council for the museum and park which they named after him. He even gave an extra £5,000 towards its conversion into a properly equipped and abundant playground for Rawtenstall children. The first Freeman of Rawtenstall (1901), he established the Richard Whitaker Charity under the terms of his will, and instigated the building of almshouses, which were first allocated in 1915, and renovated 1985.

Rawtenstall before the Edenfield bypass was built, the line of which lies just below Haslingden Road. The footpath still exists.

The river Irwell is crossed by many picturesque footbridges. This one used to be at the Holme, Townsendfold, just beyond the K Steels factory.

The office of 'greave' dates back to Saxon times. Before the introduction of magistracy into the district and before the days of Guardians of the Poor and Local Boards, Rossendale was governed by a 'Greave of the Forest'. He was the taxing officer of the district, nominated by the principal landowners and elected on an annual basis from each of the booths in turn. His other duties included those of Assessor and Recruiting Sergeant of Police, but as his functions were taken over by the development of local government, his duties gradually reduced until he was limited to the summoning of juries for the Halmot Court, held twice a year at Haslingden and whose services were made obsolete when the Law of Property (Amendment) Act of 1924 came into force. This is where the greave lived, in an area of Rawtenstall since redeveloped and named after different aspects of his duties, e.g. Constable Lee, Greave Close.

COURT.
PUBLIC NOTICE.

The next **HALMOT COURT**, or Court Baron of the Most Noble **Walter Francis Duke of Buccleuch and Queensberry**, for the several Manors of Accrington Old-hold and Accrington New-hold, is appointed to be held and kept at the **Court House in Haslingden**, on Tuesday, the 17th day of April next, at Ten o'clock in the Forenoon of the same day; and all Persons who owe suit and service at the said Court are required to attend.

The next *AUDIT* will be held at **Clitheroe Castle**, on Tuesday, the 8th Day of May, 1866.

HENRY WHITAKER, Greave of Rossendale.

FREDERIC HALL KING, PRINTER AND STATIONER, RAWTENSTALL.

This notice summoning the Hamlot Court was issued in 1866. A full list of Greaves of the Forest of Rossendale from 1559 to 1818 can be found in Thomas Newbigging's *History of the Forest of Rossendale*, though as this notice confirms, greaves continued to be appointed for many more years.

Rossendale magistrates, formed by the merger of Bacup, Rawtenstall and Haslingden justices. From Tuesday 13 November 1962, Bacup, Rawtenstall and Haslingden magistrates combined as Rossendale Magistrates, thus ending the independent towns' magistrates who in Bacup used to meet at the George & Dragon Inn until the opening in 1857 of the Court House on Bankside. The Rawtenstall Court House was in Lord Street and in Haslingden on George Street. Left to right, back row: R.W. Hill, Clifford Kenyon, Jack Edge, J.C. Whittaker, Ted Dugdale, T.C. Law, George Holt, Mrs E. Hughes, F. Holmes, Mrs D. Chanter, Roy Taylor, Mrs N. Hassan, J. Walsh, Miss N. Hodgkinson, W.H. Nuttall, Mrs F. Hoyle, E. Gibson, Dr J.T. Brooks, J. Ashworth, W. Hargreaves, F. Mitchell, Frank Haworth, Robert Driver, A.T. Good. Middle row: Hon C.K. Brooks, Mrs M.L. Hindle, Mrs D.W. Brooks, Lord Cozens Hardy, George Waddington (chairman), Mrs M. Gaskell, Mrs G. Ball, Mrs K. Butterworth, Miss B. Tattersall. Front row: B.J. Fisher, J. Ratcliffe, J. Howley (staff), I. Smith (staff), G.A. Pratt (clerk), R. Dowse (staff), Miss L. Howarth (staff), R. Howorth, A.E. Lomax.

Dawson's ironmongers' shop flourished in Barlow Street for over fifty years. The premises were originally a warehouse for Lambert Howarth, and were eventually demolished when the area was redeveloped around 1967. David Dawson, son of J.A. & E.A. Dawson, is standing at the door of the shop. His son and grandson both became well-known local photographers, whilst nephew Arthur Baldwin is a stalwart of Rossendale Groundwork.

Tup Bridge, c. 1910. The Rams Head Hotel, known locally as the 'Tup's Head' dates from the late eighteenth or early nineteenth century. The clock with roman numerals was made by Rawtenstall clockmaker J. Greaves.

Jean's hat stall in Rawtenstall indoor market, April 1994. Although popular with local shoppers, the hat stall closed when Jean Nulty, proprietress, retired after eight years in charge. She died in November 1997.

An idyllic scene at Chapel Hill, looking up Hurst Old Lane, c. 1960. Hurst Lane continues to Meadow Head, and was the old road to Lumb before the turnpike road. Just over the horizon is the old Quaker burial ground, a small rectangular plot 45ft by 36ft in which the remains of 135 persons were interred between 1663 and 1844. The bocking trade was still being carried on in August 1876 by farmers in this area for the Hardmans of Newhallhey Mills. The Waingate development ('wain' meaning wagon, 'gate' meaning road) is off to the bottom right.

Sunnyside House, Crawshawbooth. The old part of Sunnyside House dated from pre-Jacobean times, and it is believed to have been a potential escape route for supporters of Bonnie Prince Charlie. Sadly, this part of the house has been demolished, though the Jacobean ceilings said to have come from Whalley Abbey remain. An imposing 'stately home', it was for a long time the home of the Brooks family. Acquired by the Diocese of Manchester in 1963, it was used as a conference centre and retreat for more than thirty years but is currently the home of Manchester United footballer Philip Neville and his Rossendale-born wife Julie (née Killelea).

Dandy Row, Crawshawbooth, c. 1920. The row of property on the right includes Sunnyside Baptist church and the Printers Arms pub, all now demolished, with the Rushbed estate covering the area where these stood. Notorious for a dangerous S-bend in the road, this was straightened out and a new bridge designed by Lancashire County Council surveyor and bridgemaster James Drake. This is supported by a concrete archway below the road surface, through which the Limy Water flows.

Robert Lewer, seen in the doorway of his gents' clothier's shop at 560 Burnley Road, Crawshawbooth, was born in Australia after his parents had emigrated to be involved in the gold rush there. After his mother's death the family returned to England, where his father also died. Robert ended up at George Muller's Orphanage in Bristol, after which he settled in Crawshawbooth as a qualified tailor and hatter. His wife died around 1933, the shop closed shortly afterwards and he went to live with his daughter in Slough, where he died on 26 December 1946, at the age of ninety. His shop was later occupied by the Co-op and has changed hands a number of times since.

The Friends' Meeting House at Crawshawbooth is widely regarded as a quaint old Quaker place, the site of which was purchased for a mere £30, though the cost of erecting the premises on what was known in 1715 as the Old Garden was £69. Opened in May 1716, it has been in use ever since, though extended and altered in 1736. The furnishings are original. The house stands at a point where the roads from Accrington, Haslingden, Goodshaw and Newchurch converged at the old packhorse bridge over the Limy Water.

A 1987 reproduction of the front entrance.

Stoneholme Road, looking towards St John's church. The Quaker sanctuary is at the left corner and the Limy Water is behind the wall on the right. Co-operation Street crosses Stoneholme Road and the Toll Cottage is just over the bridge on the right. The area was prone to flooding in the 1930s when the bridge was blocked, but the riverbed has been lowered since.

Pilling Well, c. 1900, and still there today, sandwiched between Water Street on the left and the rear of Adelaide Street to the bottom. The river runs behind the wall, and in bad weather often used to flood the area. The well has never been known to run dry, and was the source of water for folk in the area who did not have it on tap.

Familiar view of Crawshawbooth, looking south and east from Pinner Delph. St John's Vicarage (no longer used as such) is on the middle right, a large detached stone house. Co-operation Street runs from the lower left opposite the new Black Dog, and halfway up the hill Kit Lime Gate leads on to Heightside Lane, Heightside Farm and Edge End nos 1 and 2.

Old Goodshaw Baptist chapel was originally erected in 1760 at a cost of £191 10s 4d, and was the home of the Deighn Layrocks, one of whom, John Nuttall (1716-1792) was the first pastor. Listed as an ancient monument, and in the care of the Department of the Environment, it was taken into care and restored by English Heritage. The furnishings are simple but practical, preserving a full set of box pews and galleries. On the first Sunday of every July, the 'Old Chapel Sermons' are held, reviving a local tradition suspended when the old place was declared unsafe in the 1960s. The picture dates from years back, long before recent renovations.

Goodshaw Fold is perhaps best known for two specific structures: Rehoboth chapel, set back around the corner to the top of the road, and Spewing Duck well, just off the picture to the bottom left. The houses on the left have now been demolished and the farm on the right renovated. The shadow that can just be seen in the bottom right corner is that of a house of 1610 vintage with flag floor, which has been tastefully renovated. Originally a village with some sixty-five houses and three mills (Top, Middle and Bottom factories), a considerable amount of redevelopment has taken place in Goodshaw Fold, but as a conservation area since the mid-1970s, it still retains much of its character.

Clowbridge Reservoir was constructed between 1855 and 1866 by the Haslingden and Rawtenstall Waterworks Company. This view, taken roughly a century later, is from the reservoir embankment, and apart from the loss of the factory chimney, very little has changed.

Pilgrim's Cross, Gambleside, reconstructed 1902 on the moors behind Clowbridge Reservoir. Also known as Compston's Cross after Samuel Compston, local historian and doyen of Rawtenstall Council. It is believed that this cross marks the junction where the ancient track between Rossendale and Clitheroe met the route from Preston to West Yorkshire, standing where four footpaths met.

Six
Stubbins, Edenfield and Rossendale West (including Haslingden)

'Stubbins... an attractive old village.'

'Haslingden... the westernmost of the string of overgrown industrial villages along the river Irwell.' – Nikolaus Pevsner

Five views of the Stubbins area, showing some of the vistas in this outpost of Rossendale, pictured in the 1920s.

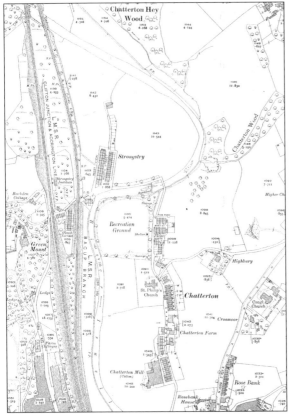

Left: map of 1930 showing the former weaving hamlets of Strongstry and Chatterton, both in secluded areas west of Bolton Road North (A676). The area now covered by the recreation ground was given as a *peace memorial* (*not* war memorial) by A.T. Porritt to Ramsbottom Urban District Council on 1 April 1922 in memory of local lads killed in the First World War, and formally opened on 14 April 1923.

Below: 'in the picture' – the massive 'frame' at Chatterton. Richard Caink crafted four sculptures, symbolic of local industry and the loom-breakers' rebellion of 1826. Sited on the Irwell Valley sculpture trail, it includes the river winding through, linking urban, rural and industrial cultures. A careful look shows broken and twisted drive-cogs, a shattered pulley, a partly uncovered sledge-hammer and a drive-belt lying idle and slack (reproduced by courtesy of Dave Clark).

Chatterton Village, 1993. In this peaceful village, the loom-breakers rioted on Wednesday 26 April 1826. Historically remembered as the Chatterton 'fight', during which forty-six looms were wrecked at the Chatterton mill owned by Thomas Aitken, and five men and a woman were fatally injured. Marks of rifle balls were visible on cottage walls in Chatterton for over 150 years, but disappeared when the houses were sandblasted. (See chapter 5 of William Turner's excellent *Riot!*, published in 1992).

Chatterton from Strongstry, showing the railway line over the river in the foreground (see map opposite). The rest of the village is to the right. On the horizon is the former Congregational manse, Greystones, occupied by successive pastors of Stubbins Congregational church from 1910 to 1953, when a smaller property was purchased for the minister.

General view of Strongstry, showing South Terrace, a line of houses built for workers at Stubbins Vale Mill, with The Cliffe (residence of the Porritt family) behind. It is now a nursing home.

Strongstry, seen looking up the river Irwell towards Rawtenstall. The two railway bridges into the village carry the line from Stubbins to Accrington and the East Lancashire Railway Preservation Society line from Bury to Rawtenstall (see map on page 96). Strongstry and Chatterton were designated a conservation area in the mid-1970s. The Rossendale Way follows an unmade track alongside the river Irwell, and soon crosses a footbridge to Chatterton village.

Scout Moor Quarries, c. 1904. This shows where setts, flags and other stone was quarried to be used in the paving of Trafalgar Square, London, and several local towns. One of the major Haslingden flag quarries, Scout Moor was leased from Lord Derby in 1830 and in its heyday employed over 300 people. Virtually derelict after the Second World War, the quarry was reopened to provide stone for the M66 motorway.

Irwell Vale centenary celebrations, 1933. From left to right: Councillor Fred Brandwood (the next mayor of Haslingden), Alderman Jerry Lord (Helmshore), Mrs W.H. Baxter (mayoress), Captain William Hudson Baxter (mayor of Haslingden), Revd William Killcross (Methodist minister), Alice Kirkham (Lancashire cotton queen), -?-, Miss Rodgers of Manchester (representing the cotton queen's employers), Mrs Elizabeth Hoyle, aged seventy-five (oldest lady in the village), -?-, -?-. The cotton queen competition was a *Daily Dispatch* initiative to boost the cotton industry after the economic down-turn in the aftermath of the First World War. No Rossendale girl ever won the title, but several cotton queens visited the valley.

The rare stained-glass windows in Edenfield ex-Primitive Methodist church (opened 12 January 1882), depicting the founders of Primitive Methodism, Bourne and Clowes. Hugh Bourne (born 3 April 1772, died 11 October 1852) made a personal visit to Rossendale in 1825, and again at the end of April 1848, but there is no specific confirmation that he actually visited Edenfield. William Clowes (born 12 March 1780, died 2 March 1851) certainly didn't.

Edenfield parish church, originally a parochial chapel-of-ease within the parish of Bury. There is a suspicion that it may have been due for dedication to St James, but no corroboration exists, so it remains the only Anglican church in Rossendale without a specific dedication. It became a parish church in its own right in 1865, though the first reference appears in the Court Roll of Tottington in 1541, when an affray in the chapel at 'Aytonfield' took place. Rebuilt in its present form in 1778, it has a leaning tower 23 inches out of true, a potential local rival to Pisa!

The popularity of the musical *The Sound of Music* in the area may have had something to do with the organising of a Tyrolean evening on 9 October 1970. It was the brainchild of Mrs H.W. Marcroft, wife of the vicar at the time, and the evening, including a four-course meal, cost 15 shillings each. A profit of £104 12s 6d resulted. Left to right, back row: Stephen Higginbotham, Michel Metcalf, Chris Higginbotham, Philip Wood, Clive Rigby, Paul Wood. Front row: Paul Metcalf, Heather Haworth, Julie Wolstenholme, Nigel Vaux. Centre front: Vicky Tattersall. A tragic footnote: Paul Metcalf, the twin brother of Michel, became a part-time fireman based at Ramsbottom, and was drowned 4 September 1999 while trying to rescue a young man from Simon's Lodge at Holcombe Brook.

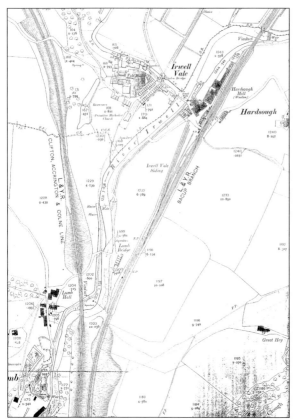

Left: a map of Irwell Vale, 1911, showing the convergence of the railway lines from Bacup on the right and from Accrington on the left.

Below: Stubbins Congregational church, demolished April 1983. Samuel and James Porritt initiated the church in 1861, making a large room available for worship in one of their mills. Building of the Gothic structure commenced in August 1865, with a spire 121ft high. It was opened for worship on 14 August 1867, the celebrated Dr R.W. Dale of Birmingham being the preacher. The building cost of £8,144 11s 4d was cleared within a year. The day and Sunday school buildings were demolished in the 1990s.

Aitken Street, Irwell Vale. The street was named after Thomas Aitken (1833-1911), owner and founder of Hardsough Mill. The chimney behind was demolished in 1986. Even today the population of Irwell Vale is only around 200, an old-world village tucked away in a quiet corner of the Rossendale Valley.

Ewood Hall, built in 1647 and still occupied, is a well-preserved and exceptional survival of type and period. The house boasts the story of a ghostly nun, and voices resembling a band of singing choristers are said to have been heard in the corner of the living room.

This panoramic vista was originally recorded *c*. 1890 by Haslingden photographers Henry & Henry from Black Isle, to the south side of Tor. In the fourteenth century Musbury Tor and its two valleys were enclosed by the then Earl of Lincoln (who was also Lord of the Manor of Tottington) as a deer park. Musbury Tor at the back overlooks Great House Farm and Tor Side Hall, bought in 1951 by the Ministry of Agriculture, Fisheries and Food and used for the next thirty years as a Government-inspired experimental farm complex. The whole estate was owned by the Porritt family who built the original Tor Side House (later extended and renamed).

Higher Mill Museum, Helmshore Road, was built by the Turner family in 1789 as a fulling mill to finish woollen cloth and was the first mill to be targeted by the loom-breakers in 1826. The mill was rebuilt 1859-60 after a disastrous fire. The archway at the eastern end, shown above, leads to the water-powered fulling mill of 1789. Higher Mill was acquired by a local trust when it became redundant in 1967. It is the only remaining mill in Rossendale which boasts a working water-wheel, 18ft in diameter, renovated and in full working order.

Park Mill at Helmshore. On the left is the former Helmshore smithy, since demolished. Park Mill now houses a cluster of industrial units. It is easy to see why the prominent and majestic Musbury Tor behind is sometimes called Rossendale's Table Mountain.

Holcombe Road, looking in the direction of Holcombe, showing the Robin Hood Inn and the 'Wood Bottom' cottages opposite that originally housed workers from nearby Higher Mill. The latter is to the left of Middle Mill currently used by Airtours. Also to be seen is a row of houses known as the Grandstand, which give a bird's eye view of Helmshore, the former Springhill Methodist church, and Helmshore Conservative Club, now a private house occupied by a former Labour councillor.

This was originally thought to relate to the Helmshore Rose Queen Festival of 1910, but is more probably the Musbury church pageant of 1911, graced by William McQuilton, who in his private life was a labourer for Haslingden Corporation, but was known throughout Lancashire for his perfect representation of 'John Bull' in pageants. His garb embraced knee breeches, high topped boots, tail coat, red or white waistcoat, silk hat to fit the part, and a John Bull pipe and walking stick. He died aged seventy-five on 8 June 1922.

Flaxmoss, Helmshore, c. 1900. The Clarence Hotel is pictured, with Anderton's grocers shop on the left. Cottages to the left were demolished and Haslingden Sports Centre was built a little lower down in 1974, to open in September 1975.

In January 1940 a terrific snowstorm hit Rossendale, blocking all the main roads and temporarily obliterating side streets. This scene on Helmshore Road looking north is opposite the road to Top o' th' Brow. Brick House Farm on the right has since been demolished.

Ravenshore Arches, looking almost due east, with Ravenshore Cottage in front and Lower Cockham Farm beyond the arches. The viaduct carried the former Stubbins-Helmshore-Accrington railway line. The stretch of water beyond the viaduct is particularly beautiful and a century ago was known as 'little Blackpool' because of the number of bathers who sported in the rock pools formed by the river Ogden.

Helmshore and Musbury church (officially known as St Thomas's and opened 1852) as seen from Holcombe Road. Tor View buildings are on the right, while the open ground behind is now the Curven Edge/Fairhill estate.

One of the local characters was Owd Edgar Maudsley, a semi-vagrant, who was described as 'retired horsethief, whiskey-spinner, liar, drinker, poacher, and blackmailer'. He lived at Black Hill Farm and used to wander round with sack on back, scavenging for whatever took his fancy. He used to call at the Co-op store at Grane, sneak a bite out of a muffin when no-one was looking, and then offer to remove the damaged goods. Local children used to sing the verse: 'There is a man from Haslingden, Who's called the Mayor of Grane. No matter where you see him, He's always dressed the same. He has a trilby hat on, And spats up to his knees, And if you go too near him, He'll cover you with fleas.'

A group of villagers on the ruins of Chapel Row during demolition, c. 1960. Chapel Row was built along the lane leading from Stoney Rake to Hartley House and Rothwell Fold in the early years of the nineteenth century, when handloom weaving was at its height. These cottages were built back to earth, with the Wesleyan chapel, built in 1815 at a cost of £700, at one end. This was the first place of worship in the Grane Valley but was demolished 1956.

At the top end of the Grane Valley is Calf Hey reservoir. Constructed to supply water to Bury, this was completed in 1861 at a cost of £12,000, not counting the £9,000 needed to repair the damage caused in April 1856 when a massive landslide from the embankment demolished a house which at the time stood in the way. Note Fairy Glen to the right and Cribden in the background.

Crow Trees Cottage, which is still there today, although other property in the background has been demolished. Across the road from the original St Stephen's church, Crow Trees was originally a seventeenth-century yeoman's farm.

The largest and last of the three reservoirs at Haslingden Grane, Ogden Reservoir was opened in March 1912 by the mayor of Bury. Below its waters lie the remains of Rothwell Fold, Calf Hey Mill, and Broad Holden Mill. Note on the left the Duke of Wellington hostelry, built in the early 1800s to serve travellers on the new turnpike road through Grane, and in the middle the water treatment plant.

Fairy Glen. Situated to the south-west of Calf Hey reservoir, this attractive wooded clough was originally dubbed 'Th' hell hoile' by old Graners, but a local clergyman felt this an inappropriate description, and re-christened it. Legend suggests that a fairy named Silverwing was sent by Oberon and Titania into Lancashire, where the fairy glen was discovered by the side of the river Ogden. The King immediately claimed it as his summer residence, which is why the fairies can only be seen when the sun is at its zenith. Therefore it is called, not the fairies' glen but the Fairy Glen, to mark the great honour of the place.

Jottings

Top: St Stephen's church, Grane. This impressive building was completed in 1867 at Crow Trees in the Grane Valley $1\frac{1}{4}$ miles away, in the centre of what was then a populous and thriving community. But in 1883 Bury & District Water Board began to plan an extension of the catchment areas of their reservoirs at Grane. Calf Hey had already been completed in 1861, and two further reservoirs were to be constructed. As old Graners moved out, church attendances declined, and in 1910 a mission room was built at Holden Wood. In February 1921, Major David Halstead gifted a one-acre site (then being used as a football field) for the building of a church. In 1923 Manchester Diocesan authorities approved the dismantling of St Stephen's church at Crow Trees and rebuilt at the new Lane Ends site, where it was consecrated by the Rt Revd Percy Mark Herbert, first bishop of the new Blackburn Diocese that came into being in 1926. Unfortunately, dwindling congregations resulted in the final closure of the church for worship in 1986. Eventually, the premises were bought and turned into the tasteful Holden Wood Antiques, open every day. The stained glass windows are still *in situ*.

Above left: the Runic stone cross in the old graveyard of the former church in the Grane Valley bears the following inscription: 'On this site formerly stood the Parish Church of St Stephen Haslingden Grane which was built in the year 1864AD. It was taken down stone by stone and rebuilt on a site $1\frac{1}{4}$ miles nearer Haslingden and reconsecrated on the 22nd May 1927 by the Right Rev Dr Herbert Lord Bishop of Blackburn'.

A vista of Haslingden in 1820, looking towards Carter Place from St James' parish church. To the right of centre is Paghouse Mill, destroyed by fire in May 1878 and scene of a massive explosion in 1905.

Tor Mile race, 22 July 1963. Pictured, from left to right: Brian Hall (Manchester & District Harriers), winner of the club race in a record 8 minutes 1.4 seconds; Chris Aspin, secretary of the Helmshore Local History Society and well-known local historian; Alf Bedford, aged 89 at the time, and the oldest member of Helmshore Local History Society; Michael Eastwood, winner of the Tor Mile local race. Alf Bedford (1874-1965), signalman at Helmshore station for forty-three years, used to play an accordian, and when he was a little lad, his father brought home a fiddle he had bought for half a crown – friends collected the 1s 6d needed to buy a bow! In later life Alf was a member of the Helmshore Prize Band. A keen cyclist till the age of eighty-three, he began with a penny-farthing and progressed to a Kangaroo (the first chain-driven bike). The Tor Mile race dates from before the First World War, and involved a 800ft climb to the top of Musbury and back. The race was revived 1958-1965.

Haslingden Borough Council 1973-74, with their chief officers, pictured in the council chamber in November 1973. Left to right, back row: David Tennant, George Wellock, Harry Uren (street lighting foreman), Tom Maddox (baths superintendent), Bill D.Y. Carruthers (parks superintendent), Jim Rishton, Alderman Albert Bussey, Jack Stafford, Donald Valentine, Tom Illingworth, Geoff Hallam, Ivor Cooper, George Worswick (mayor's attendant), Geoff Ormerod, Hubert Sanderson, Jack Hollows (chief public health inspector), William G. Wood (borough engineer and surveyor), Brian Yorke, Cliff Billings (borough treasurer). Front row: Alderman Mrs Gertrude Warburton, Councillor Dorothy Ramsden, R.B. McMillan (town clerk), Alderman Donald Butterworth (mayor), Councillor Tom B. Fisher (deputy mayor), Alderman Roy Woolley. Eight other members of the council were absent at the time.

This compact council chamber on Bury Road served for the whole life of the Borough of Haslingden (1891-1974), before which it was the former home of the Woodcock family of solicitors. Used by Rossendale Borough Council for some years after local government reorganization, it has now been demolished.

This stained-glass window, formerly in Haslingden Municipal Offices, proudly displays Haslingden's motto: NOTHING WITHOUT LABOUR. It now reposes in Whitaker Park Museum.

115

Robert Scott's birthplace of 14 Peel Street, Haslingden, bears a blue plaque commemorating Rossendale's only recipient of the Victoria Cross. He joined the 1st Battalion of the Manchester Regiment in 1895 along with his elder brother James, who was to be awarded an OBE in 1919. At the outbreak of the Boer War Robert went to South Africa and in January 1900 played a decisive role in the defence of Ladysmith. He and Private Pitts of Blackburn held the Caesar's Camp outpost for fifteen hours, during which period all their comrades were killed. The two had no food or water and were under constant shell-fire. The only Rossendale man to be featured on a cigarette card (no. 83 in the James Taddy series of VC heroes) Robert Scott lived the last forty years of his life in County Down, where he died aged eighty-six on 22 February 1961.

Haslingden Baths, interior. Opened 22 August 1936 on East Bank Avenue, with depths varying from 3ft 6 inches to 7ft 9 inches, and 75ft long by 30ft wide.

This firm, J.S. Cordingley, was established in 1882 by champion racing cyclist John Stancliffe Cordingley, who after selling furniture turned to selling cycles, the 'Rossendalian' being most popular with cycle clubs. Cordingley's sold the first car purchased in Haslingden, the first Model T Ford. The firm ran for three generations until Jack Cordingley's retirement in July 1981. The photograph depicts his shop on Blackburn Road around 1900. Later he acquired the former Primitive Methodist chapel on Deardengate, from which Cordingley's operated till the retirement of the last owner.

'Phones : Works 2 y ; Residence No. 102.   Telegrams : "Cordingley, Haslingden.

"The MOTOR BAZAAR OF THE NORTH."

Works and Garage :
NUTTALL ST. and QUEEN ANNE ST.

Offices & Showrooms :
———DEARDENGATE.———

SIDDELEY-
DEASY,
LANCHESTER,
AUSTIN,
CROSSLEY,
AND BELSIZE
CARS.

ARROL-
JOHNSTON,
KRIT,
SWIFT AND
FLANDERS
CARS.

J. S. Cordingley,
Automobile Engineer.

IENTS' CARS ARE ONLY DRIVEN
OUR STAFF AT CLIENTS' OWN
K AND RESPONSIBILITY.

PLEASURE CARS AND MOT
CHAR-A-BANCS FOR HI

Haslingden,

The headed paper dates from 1914.

St James' church, with an angel-topped tombstone in the foreground. St James' church dominates the Haslingden skyline and the surrounding countryside from its elevated position in the oldest part of town. The 'top church' for some 725 years, with origins possibly Saxon. The church has many links with the past, including old stocks and an even older parish chest. At the foot of the tower is a stone believed by some to have been the base of a Saxon cross. The pinnacles were removed in the interests of safety and the watchful angel is now in safe keeping inside the church after vandal activity.

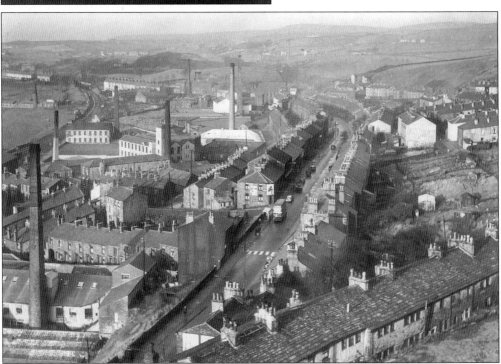

Blackburn Road, Haslingden, seen from St James' church tower. Mitchells' tripe works are on the left of the railway line. Houses on the mid-right were demolished in the 1960s and the West View estate built. Buildings still standing include the Britannia Mill (CWS slipper works), and Union Mill (Robinsons), but the other mills featured here – Hazel Mill, Clough End Mill, Carr Mill and Albert Mill – are now but memories.

Cob Castle and Windy Harbour from St James' church tower. Blackburn Road is in the foreground, the railway behind. Todd Hall Farm is right of centre with Carrs (now demolished to form the line of the bypass). Roundhill Road leading towards Blackburn can be seen on the right.

Haslingden's railway line, as recorded in the 1940s, showing the station and St James' church in the distance, and also Baxter's Brewery, which is apparently even higher than the church! This was on Hud Rake, and was demolished when West View was built. Note Mitchell's tripe works on the right edge, and count the mill chimneys – there are none left now! Also notice the level-crossing gate linking the isolated Carrs with the Blackburn Road area of town.

Hutch Bank in the early years of the twentieth century. On the horizon is Hutch Bank Quarry, exporting setts and building stone to all parts of the country, where they were widely used for paving. Note Spring Vale Mill, and Plantation Mill built 1881. The famous local runner 'Choppy' (James Edward Warburton) worked at Hutch Bank Mill till the 1860s but the mill boiler blew up 15 October 1875, causing £3,000 worth of damage. There was one fatality. Flip Row linked Charles Lane and the mill, passing under the railway, just beyond which was the Dyers' Arms, familiarly known as the 'Flip'. Five water pumps supplied the stuff of life to local homes.

During 1940 four enemy bombs fell on Haslingden, but fortunately no local casualties were caused. It is recorded that folk in Haslingden contributed more National Savings per head of population than almost any other industrial town, £11 5s 0d per head. This detailed picture shows Mrs Evans and Mrs Parker at a WVS stall on Deardengate during Aluminium Appeal Week 1943, aluminium being recyclable even then.

The Great Blizzard at the end of January 1940 resulted in the Manchester to Colne train running into this five-foot drift at Carter Place Cutting. Half the complement of passengers chose to walk to Accrington via the railway embankment, the rest were found overnight accommodation locally. The line was closed for almost a week. Note the third-class carriages.

Royal visit to Haslingden, 8 March, 1945. Pictured, from left to right, are: Alderman A.S. Watson (mayor), King George VI, Alderman William Boyson (deputy mayor), Queen Elizabeth, Mrs Boyson (deputy mayoress), Alderman T.F. Haworth (the longest-serving member of Haslingden Council with thirty-three years' service, including twenty-three as chairman of the library committee), Mrs S.A. Jennings of Park Lane View, Holden Wood, a widow with six sons and a nephew on active service (her mother had once been presented to Queen Victoria). The royal visit lasted all of ten minutes, in the grounds of Central Council School on East Bank Avenue. Afterwards the King and Queen went on to Ramsbottom via Ewood Bridge. Three years later, the Queen passed through Haslingden yet again en route from Blackburn to Rochdale during a visit to the cotton mills of Lancashire.

Cissy Green's shop on Deardengate, with current manager Barry Howorth. The shop is believed to date back 200 years and is best remembered for the legendary Sarah Green, better known as Cissy, who married Ernest Ashworth and eventually lived in Manchester Road until her death at the age of eighty around 1960. The Saturday lunch of many folk was often a Cissy Green pie. Changes of name mattered little, customers always called the shop Cissy Green's and the current owner was happy to respond to local demand, restoring the name in honour of the bubbly lady with grey hair who gave the deservedly popular shop its reputation.

Celebrating the fiftieth anniversary of the end of the Second World War in Europe, 8 May 1945. Pictured, from left to right, are: Steven Hartley, so far the only Chief Executive of Rossendale Borough Council, 1994-95 Mayor Bob Wilkinson, retired firefighter, and mayor's attendant Bob Trickett, who at the end of April 2000 retired after thirty years service as mayor's chauffeur and later attendant.

Haslingden railway station looking towards Burnley. The town's bypass follows the line of the railway, which closed to passenger traffic on 5 November 1960. Cross Street North is behind the tallest chimney, Sherfin is on the skyline, and Wesley Methodist church (1884-1970) to the left of the first chimney. At the foot of the picture is Bridge Street, locally known as Donkey Row.

Henry Stephenson, historian, botanist, geologist and copious diarist, was born 17 November 1842 in Oswaldtwistle, educated at Foxhill Bank and Accrington before moving to Haslingden in 1854 and taking up residence at 14 Bury Road. After a few jobs in local mills, he was invited to join the teaching staff at St James' church school in 1866 and in 1875 became headmaster there until retiring at the early age of forty-seven. He died in 1922. His notebooks give valuable historical and genealogical information on local families. He was pictured by Haslingden photographer John J. Rishton.

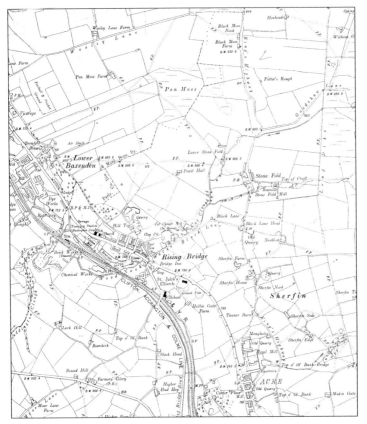

The King's Highway is believed to be of Saxon origin, and has certainly been in use since Norman times. Its name derives from the authority of the King, in whose name the lord of the manor at Clitheroe maintained the highway. As the powers of the manors declined, so did the condition of this highway, resulting in numerous complaints, until in 1789 John Metcalf's new turnpike road from Bury to Whalley made the King's Highway redundant as a major route, though the line of the Accrington bypass, completed 1985, follows the old Highway quite closely.

In the 1871 census, John McKenzie's birthplace was stated to be on board a British ship! Of Scottish origin, he could not speak English properly, nor even Scotch correctly. A pedlar by trade, his by-name was Dom Ady or Long-de-Dong, and he divided his time between Haslingden and Accrington. His name derived from the refrain he used to chant while walking along the streets, which sounded like Long my Tongue or Long de Dong, but apparently was descriptive of the sulphur matches he hawked around as 'long and strong'. An old army veteran, he had fought in Spain and ended up in the Scots Greys at the Battle of Waterloo. He died at his lodgings in High Street, Haslingden, on 24 October 1872 aged 100, and was interred in St James' churchyard.

"OLD LONG-DE DONG"

Looking down Rising Bridge Road past Stonefold School.

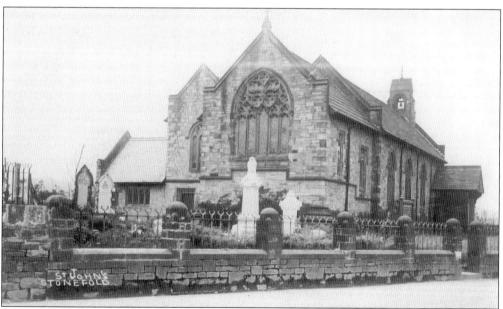

St John's church, Stonefold. In 1844, Rising Bridge comprised the Bridge Inn and a few houses in and around Worsley Street. Clerically the area was served by the Wesleyan Sunday school of 1835 and the Anglican equivalent in 1836. By 1874 the latter was considered too small and damp, and five years later an iron church and school were built at a cost of £600. Five years later Miss Martha Turner of Carter Place funded a permanent stone structure, the foundation stone being laid by her nephew on 13 September 1884. St John's was consecrated 21 May 1886. Originally served by clergy from St James', Haslingden, Stonefold parish's first vicar was Revd Richard Parker (curate of St James', Haslingden), appointed 1889 and vicar for twenty-six years until his early death aged fifty-three on 19 April 1915, in practice the longest-serving vicar of St John's Stonefold. Worship was suspended in 2001.

Holland's Pie Factory has operated from several different addresses – Deardengate, then Church Street, St John Street, and finally Baxenden, where Walter Holland acquired the old industrial mill in 1936. Deliveries were made by horse and cart till 1927 when the first delivery van was bought, and by 1938 there were twenty vans making regular deliveries around Lancashire, when their total workforce was about 100. Walter Holland, whose father founded the firm, was a racing cyclist in 1890s, and died 3 August 1942 aged seventy-one. In May 1949 the firm changed hands and there is no longer a Holland on the staff. Production has risen from 100,000 pies a week in 1925 to nearly $1\frac{1}{2}$ million pies a week in 2002. The largest employer in the Rossendale Valley, there are 500 employees at a firm which corners 85% of the north-west fresh pie market, and has found official favour with football clubs ranging from Accrington Stanley to Norwich City. The tall chimney was demolished May 1983.

The succulent pies still appreciated 150 years after the foundation of the firm.

The floods of July 1964 caused considerable local havoc, as this wreckage of a Ford Anglia car near Baxenden station signal box illustrates. This signal box (and the station), 750ft above sea-level, at the top of a 1:40 climb from Accrington, lie within Rossendale, but the Five Arches viaduct belongs to Hyndburn. In Helmshore, over 3 inches of rain fell in less than an hour.

Before a turnpike linked Haslingden and Accrington, the hamlet of Stonefold was on the King's Highway, and was cited September 1623 in court rolls illustrating the partition of Henheads Pasture. The King's Highway crossed the moor beneath the slopes of Cribden, linking Haslingden to the ecclesiastical centre of medieval Whalley. John Wesley's Journal for 22 April 1788 made a telling comment: '…we went through still more wonderful roads to Haslingden. They were sufficient to lame any horses, and shake any carriage in pieces. NB: I will never attempt to travel these roads again till they are effectually mended!' Black Moss was an area of bogland and peat, where cotton sedge grew profusely in springtime. The farm, pictured in 1927, was nearer to Accrington than to the Stonefold area of Haslingden.

The Haweswater Aqueduct, constructed 1949-54 to enable drinking water from the Lake District reservoir to reach Manchester, has since 1954 carried about a hundred million gallons of water per day at a speed of about two miles an hour through the aqueduct which channels the water southwards. The shaft at Rising Bridge, sunk March 1950, was 332ft deep. Eventually lined with concrete, the smooth finished tunnel was 8ft 6 inches in diameter, big enough to drive a car through!